WHAT CAUSED THE BIG BANG?

To Steve Hasan,

I'm your biggest fan!

Regards,

Jeffrey August

WHAT CAUSED THE BIG BANG?

Consciousness and Enlightenment in the Internet Age and Beyond

Jeffrey Augustine

http://www.jeffreyaugustine.com

CONTENTS

INVOCATION

God disunifies into the gray-pink vaults
into the marbled heavens of dream
into the synaptic fires of flesh
and the allure of worlds in one verse.

There is an endless hall of mirrors
an endless book of verse
desire without limitation
within this limitation of birth.

Seeing, thinking, and feeling
this breath and the next
my heart, my very heart
this passion, this unrest.

INTRODUCTION TO DISUNIFICATION COSMOLOGY

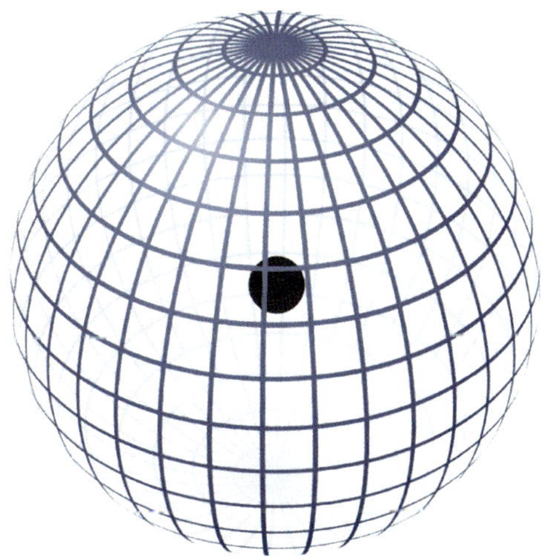

The account of Divine Creation as told in the Bible is an unconvincing old story, a relic from the religious past.

Likewise, the modern atheistic claim that the Big Bang just spontaneously happened is equally unconvincing unless one is an atheist.

This book offers a Third Option, a striking new description of the event in Infinity that caused the Big Bang.

The event that caused the Big Bang is called *the Disunification*.

The Disunification was a cosmological event.

What does the word "cosmology" mean?

Cosmology is a compound word formed from two Greek words:

- ❖ **Kósmos**, a word that refers to our Universe and all of the forms, processes, and beings that arise therein.

- ❖ **Lógos**, a word used to describe a specialized body of knowledge that offers insights into the ultimate nature of Reality. The word "Logos" is used because what we teach is specialized, transformative, and easy to understand. There is no gnosis, no secret knowledge involved in this book. What we present is philosophy with a fascinating view of spirituality and physics.

Disunification Cosmology is the study of the event that caused the Big Bang and its implications for human Consciousness. It is also referred to as **Day Teaching** for reasons that will become evident. The two terms are synonymous.

This book is the introductory text for Day Teaching.

NEW TERMS AND CONCEPTS

Several new terms and concepts are introduced in the text.

A glossary is provided in the back of the book containing the definitions of these new terms and concepts.

Two examples are ***Disunification*** and ***Primal Matter***. These two terms used in a sentence give a sense of their meaning:

> "The Disunification describes the actual event and force that 'disunified' the Primal Matter from Infinity and then evolved it into all of the forms, processes, and beings in our Universe."

The Primal Matter and its conversion and evolution into everyone and everything in our entire Universe are the key subjects of this book. Primal Matter is of particular interest, as it pertains to Consciousness and your own Soul.

Chapter One

The Black Pearl

THE PRIMAL MATTER

Many popular science writers are fond of telling their readers that everything in our entire Universe was once contained in a tiny particle, or a singularity, that was smaller than the period at the end of this sentence.

This tiny particle is said to have unaccountably exploded into our Universe in an event called the Big Bang. This tiny particle contained the Primal Matter, for out of it came everything in our Universe.

This tiny particle is the **Black Pearl**.

Our Universe exploded into existence from a center point.

This is illustrated by using a sphere with four arrows extending from it as shown below.

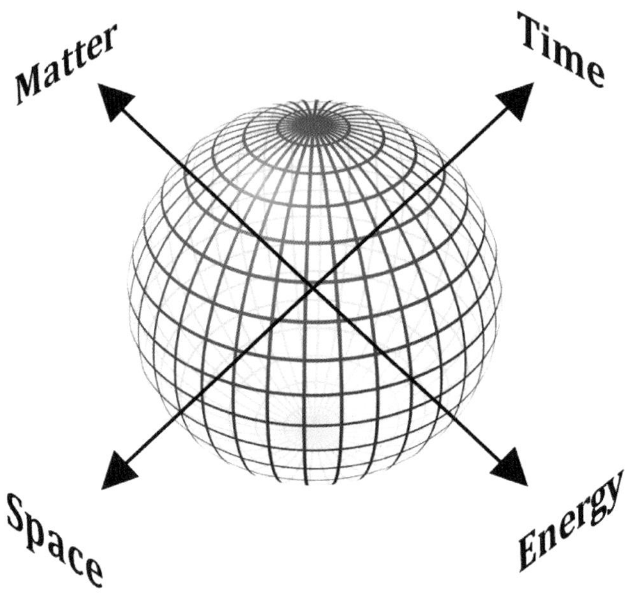

Four basic physical properties in our Universe that were disunified from the Black Pearl in the Big Bang.

At the end of each arrow is a label with various forms of Primal Matter that disunified from the Black Pearl.

This type of diagram is called a "four corner diagram," several of which are used throughout this book to illustrate the Disunification.

Inasmuch as everything in our Universe disunified from a tiny Black Pearl, or singularity, one simple question must be asked:

Where did the Black Pearl that exploded into our Universe come from?

This question requires asking a related question:

How did all of the Primal Matter get packaged into the tiny Black Pearl in the first place?

To answer these questions requires a very important distinction:

Infinity and our Universe are two different domains

According to astrophysical research, our Universe came into existence 13.75 billion years ago.

This means that our Universe has not existed forever.

Since we know for certain that our Universe came into existence at a certain point in time, we can conclude that our Universe is sub-Infinite.

This is true because if our Universe were Infinite, it would never have had a finite beginning 13.75 billion years ago.

The only logical place for the Primal Matter to have come from is Infinity, for Infinity existed prior to our Universe.

INFINITY & OUR SUB-INFINITE UNIVERSE

In ***The Physics of Immortality***, Dr. Frank Tipler asserts:

> "The universe is defined to be the totality of all that exists, the totality of reality. Thus, by definition, if God exists, He/She is either the universe or part of it."[1]

I take exception with the definition that the "universe is defined to be the totality of all that exists" and instead maintain that Infinity and our Universe are two separate and different domains.

A strategic notion of this work is that our Universe – and all other universes in the Multiverse - are sub-Infinite and are "sourced" by Infinity. The distinction between Infinity and our Universe has two key implications explored in this book:

❖ Our Universe and all universes in the Multiverse are sub-Infinite and disunified from Infinity

❖ All Divinities, Gods, Goddesses, angels, demons, humans, religions, and all other expressions in Consciousness are sub-Infinite and disunified from Infinity

This book reveals the beginning of our Universe from both sides: From Infinity and from what we see on this side as a Big Bang.

You passed from Infinity into our Universe during the event that caused the Big Bang. You can remember what happened. This book will help you to remember.

"Remembering Infinity" is an important part of this work, for in remembering we gain an enormous perspective on our Universe and everything that arises within Consciousness. We can transcend many barriers in ourselves when we remember and understand our true nature.

---

[1] Tipler, Frank. The Physics of Immortality Modern Cosmology: God and the Resurrection of the Dead. Knopf Doubleday Publishing Group, London, 1997.

THE DOORS OF PERCEPTION

"If the doors of perception were cleansed everything would appear to man as it is, infinite. For man has closed himself up, till he sees all things through narrow chinks of his cavern."

- William Blake

I have seen for myself what William Blake and so many others have seen.

I have seen and experienced Infinity.

The Ancient of Days, William Blake (1757-1827)

By cleansing the doors of perception, you too will be able to see Infinity. Once you see Infinity for yourself, you can profoundly shift your sense of identity.

For many people, this shift will be very liberating because it frees them from painful identities and all of the false and unexamined beliefs that keep these painful identities locked in place.

How does a person "cleanse the doors of perception" in order to see Infinity?

One of the main tools we use to cleanse perception is **deconstruction**. Deconstruction simply means that we take various things apart to see what they are made of.

One thing we find in deconstruction is that there are many self-created barriers to perception. These barriers often take the form of an identity to which we cling when this is not needed and in fact interferes with perception.

After we identify the event that caused the Big Bang, we will deconstruct the ways in which Consciousness disunified from Infinity in completely unsuspected ways that have profoundly affected human identity.

Once you discover what caused the Big Bang, surprising new answers to the classic questions fall into place:

1. Why our Universe came into existence

2. What caused the Big Bang

3. Why Consciousness is an intrinsic part of our Universe

4. Why there are so many different versions of God

5. Why there are so many different and competing religions

6. Why Good and Evil exist

7. Who you fundamentally are after all of your false identities are stripped away

8. What happens after you die

9. The Purpose of Life

10. How to find meaning in your own life

Your knowledge and understanding of Life and the Universe will expand as a result of reading this book. This teaching is new and profound; it has never been known until now. And while I am a Master Mason and a Knight Templar, this book and my work are not Masonic in nature.

ARISING

What does "arising" mean?

Arising is very important, for it refers the totality of that which is manifest and appears in our Universe and within you.

You can generally see, feel, measure, know, and experience most of that which is arising within yourself and the world around you.

When something in you or around you is arising and you don't know what it is, you could become curious, disturbed, or fascinated, depending upon how you react or what you perceive an unknown thing to be. To the extent that you cannot see or know that which is arising, you are unaware.

We innately want to know what things are.

You might not know what certain things are, but they are nevertheless arising.

For example, who are the people that arise in your dreams?

There is no one single answer to this question.

Divinities, angels, phantoms, reveries, demons, figments of your imaginations, and so many other things arise in your dreams.

Quarks, Higgs bosons, and quantum strangeness arise in our Universe.

All of the universes in the Multiverse and all of their possible histories arise.

You will see the common source from which all things arise.

Chapter Two

INFINITY VS. MONOTHEISM

The word "monotheism" comes from compounding two Greek words:

- ❖ *Mono*, which means *one*
- ❖ *Theos*, which means God

Monotheism is the belief that there is only one true God and that this God created the Heavens and the Earth.

The three main monotheistic religions of the world are Judaism, Christianity, and Islam. Because these three religions all began with the biblical patriarch Abraham, they constitute what is called **Abrahamic Monotheism**.

Judaism, Christianity, and Islam have spawned numberless and warring denominations, sects, schools, and schismatic groups.

Monotheism has caused endless religious warfare and bloodshed.

We bypass the entire monotheistic argument altogether by pointing out that something is missing in the doctrines of Judaism, Christianity, Islam, and every other monotheistic religion.

What is missing is the realization of Infinity.

Infinity and monotheism are two completely different things altogether.

Monotheism is absolutely sub-infinite for the simple reason that its "God" falls fall short of Infinity.

While monotheistic religions consider God to pervade the endless light years of the Empyrean through spiritual omnipresence, they nevertheless limit God when it comes to Good and Evil.

The Creator-God of monotheistic religions is claimed to be larger than our Universe and yet he is presented as being morally finite, i.e. he contains no Evil or shadow of turning.

Monotheists do not permit their God to be truly infinite in all ways, for to be truly Infinite would mean that their God must be both Good and Evil. The conceptual problem here is simple. If Evil is excluded from God, then God cannot be Infinite. To exclude *anything* from Infinity leaves us with something less than Infinity.

Monotheistic religions cannot cope with the implications of an infinite God in whom there is Good and Evil, Light and Darkness, Male and Female, and all other polarities and contradictions. Monotheistic religions are therefore sub-Infinite.

Monotheistic religions are utterly blind to Infinity and to any real sense of an Infinite God.

Worse, the God of monotheism is said to authorize his "Chosen People" to kill infidels and unbelievers as needed, and often by gruesome means, as the world saw on 9/11. We want none of this. In fact, monotheism as a "model of human Consciousness" must end, and is, in fact, coming to its historical and evolutionary end.

THE INFINITE SOURCE CONSCIOUSNESS

In this book, the concept of "God" as a person is deconstructed and reconsidered altogether.

"God" is understood to be Infinity itself. Therefore, God is not an individual person or a single identity.

Rather, God is the ***Infinite Source Consciousness*** that disunified into sentient beings in our Universe.

The illustration below offers one example of the how the Infinite Source Consciousness disunified into the **Resident Consciousness** in our Universe:

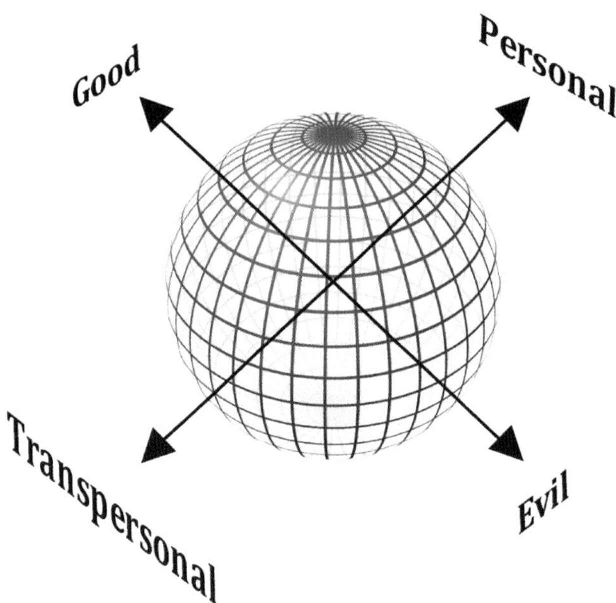

The Infinite Source Consciousness spans an endless range from the *Personal* to the *Transpersonal*.

What do the terms Personal and Transpersonal mean?

Personal Consciousness

- Personal Consciousness refers to a definite identity – to the "I" that you experience yourself as being. You normally link your sense of "I" to your feelings and thoughts when in fact you don't need to identify with your feelings and thoughts at all. The ups and downs in life can become more intense when one thinks they are their feelings and thoughts. This "false identification" is explored throughout this book.

- Personal Consciousness spans the expanse from feeling existential dread to experiencing being one with the Universe. In either case, there is an "I" present experiencing some problem or bliss within a sense of self.

- In Personal Consciousness, a sense of duality and dilemma is experienced. This is perhaps most acutely felt in the perceived duality between Good and Evil. This duality occurs when one does not understand the full range of Consciousness.

- A very common human desire is to only want to be Good and to have no signs or traces of Evil within. However, we all have Evil thoughts and desires within. A person may therefore embrace various religious or psychological strategies in an attempt to fend off Evil and purge themselves of Evil. You will see why this is unnecessary if you simply expand your sense of self and do not act upon Evil.

Transpersonal Consciousness

- Transpersonal Consciousness refers to Consciousness as it arises prior to any identity or "I." No identities or separate selves arise in Transpersonal Consciousness.

- The state or condition of Transpersonal Consciousness has been described as Nothingness in Eastern spiritual disciplines.

- In its blissful form, Transpersonal Consciousness can be experienced as a temporal state of Nirvana in which one simply is Awareness itself and has no need for any identity of any kind.

Good and Evil are part of the vast range, or spectrum, of the Infinite Source Consciousness that was disunified into human Consciousness. Therefore:

- ❖ Evil does not exist because Adam and Eve sinned against God in the Garden of Eden.

- ❖ Evil does not exist due to any defect or flaw within human Consciousness.

- ❖ All of us contain Good and Evil and are responsible for our own conduct and the consequences of our choices.

- ❖ Religious pronouncements about morality and Evil are not meaningful to the nonreligious world.

GOD IS INFINITY

God is Infinity and contains everything

Infinity is the Primal Matter.

The Primal Matter contains two interrelated streams. These two streams are bound into a state of Unity within Infinity.

These two interrelated streams are called:

- ❖ **Life Awareness**

- ❖ **Life Energy**

The acronym for the Life Energy and Life Awareness is **LELA**.

LELA is our personification of Infinity. "She" is Infinity and contains all things bound into a State of Unity.

LELA is the Infinite Source Consciousness of our universes and of all universes in the Multiverse.

LELA has no central identity and is in fact the source of all identities.

As Infinity, LELA includes all identities that sum to the Infinite Transpersonal Consciousness.

LELA is Monolithic Infinity.

She is not a sub-Infinite monotheistic God but is rather the ultimate source of all sub-Infinite monotheistic Gods.

LELA is not bound to the descriptions of any human religion.

Indeed, the phenomena of human religions and their Divinities occur as a result of the Infinite Transpersonal Consciousness disunifying into religions, religious identities, and all other identities.

LELA[2] is used as a feminine noun in order to offer a contrast to the masculine God of biblical monotheism.

However, Infinity includes all expressions of sex and gender within its Unity.

Sex, gender, and sexual preference become expressed in Disunification, as does everything else.

A sharp break is made between Infinity and monotheism in order to free people from the psychological and spiritual bondage inherent in monotheistic religion.

---

[2] For spiritually inclined readers, Appendix A contains a list of LELA's attributes. Appendix B contains a list of the Powers of Infinity.

Chapter Three

Angeles Crest Highway, Near Mount Wilson, Southern California
J. Augustine

A DRIVE IN THE MOUNTAINS:

HOW I CREATED

DISUNIFICATION COSMOLOGY

Here's how I unpackaged, unfolded, and then created Disunification Cosmology form within my very own Soul. It all happened during a drive up into the San Gabriel Mountains of Southern California.

One cold Saturday morning, I found myself a passenger in a sleek sports car that was sprinting like a steel blue panther up an old winding mountain road. The once smooth black of the road had faded over many years of freezing nights, snow runoff, and hot summers into a coarse brown speckled strip leading up into the tall timber and blazing blue sky above Southern California.

My friend knew this old road. He knew how to maneuver his swift, radial-pawed beast up the lush mountainside. As we neared the crest of the mountain, he downshifted and accelerated. Blue steel blurred against the backdrop of granite and pine as the car growled and tore around a hairpin turn towards the next gravel-strewn switchback that had no guardrail.

I could feel the vibrations of the powerful rear engine rise and fall through the black leather bucket seat into which I strapped. The sharp, square dashboard was low and the large windshield flowed seamlessly down onto the sloped hood. Except for the forward window posts, I had unlimited visibility for 180 degrees.

Cool jazz was playing on the stereo.

The weak winter sun shone through the pale bronze tinting on the windows. Neither of us spoke. The drive was one of those intensely sensual road trips that invited you to get lost in the experience it offered. Therefore, we did. Each of us intuitively accepted the experience's invitation to lose ourselves in its moment.

Why not get lost?

This particular experience would only happen once in the world's lifetime and it wanted us to enjoy it for the short time it would be alive. We were thus both lost in our own worlds; my friend in driving his sports car up a challenging mountain road, and I in drinking in the sky, the snow on the side of the road, and the towering evergreens anchored deeply into the San Gabriel Mountains of Southern California.

The soundtrack to these lush sensations was being played through a stereo system so sweet that it felt like you were living inside of the music itself.

I looked through the side passenger window down into the valley far below and saw thick white clouds swirling up from its floor. The jagged clouds climbed up into the freezing sky and grabbed at it like the wispy fingers of a ghost reaching for a life it had once known.

"Don't you remember when we dreamed all of this?" the experience asked me.

I had never had the impression of another speaking inside of my head, but this was clearly the voice of another. The voice had authority and dignity.

"Don't you remember when we dreamed all of this?" The voice asked me once again.

I suddenly went into a state of Satori, a state I had experienced before. During Satori, the Mind is muted; none of the mental chatter it superimposes on the present moment can be heard.

Satori is among the finest peak states available in human life. Its rarity makes it all the more desirable and elusive. You cannot summon such a state. Rather, as it did during the drive, it summoned me to its silent purity. It did so for a definite purpose and the words you are now reading reflect that purpose.

I suddenly flashed back to some distant time and place in which I was huddled with a countless group of others as we peered into a Dreaming Pool up from which swirled clouds like those I had just seen in the valley. Within the depths of the pool, we saw visions of the earth. "Don't you remember? We said that we would have sky, waters, lands, trees, families, and friends," the voice said to me.

The vision of the Dreaming Pool moment was remarkable and continued for some time. The essence of the moment was that I knew I had something new to communicate about the way in which our Universe was brought into existence.

The next day found me seated in front of my computer thinking about what had happened to me.

It did not make sense, for I did not know about the origins of the Universe beyond the possibilities that it had been created by God or that it had come into existence through a mysterious naturalistic Big Bang and that God did not exist.

Since the time of Darwin, that brilliant, sensitive genius, the options for explaining from whence we came have been either Divine creation or a godless evolution that began in the Big Bang.

Of course, there has always been the option of saying that God used evolution.

Yet, that is an odd form of metaphysical negotiation: why would the God of the Bible need to experiment with evolution?

Why would the Judeo-Christian God, especially with that his vaunted creative powers, use evolution?

Using "trial and error" evolution is hardly Godlike after all.

As I thought about this conflict between creation and evolution, I suddenly understood the Disunification. In an instant I saw everything and typed the phrase:

The Disunification of Energy and Awareness

That is when I quit drawing abstract architectural images with my Rapidograph pens every day and started writing instead.

My drawings were pre-Disunification Cosmology works wherein I was exploring the resolution of lines.

My drawing ***Temples Unfolding from Infinity*** (shown on the next page) prefigured my cosmology.

I drew this particular drawing long before I ever went for that drive in the mountains. This is one of my favorite drawings as it has so much personal meaning. The drawing is read from right to left.

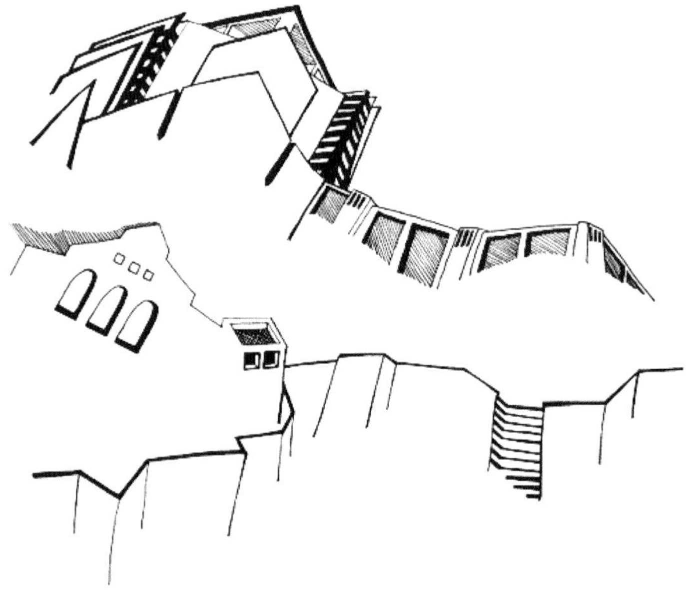

Temples Unfolding from Infinity

J. Augustine

Once I realized the Disunification, I spent a long time creating, evolving, and disunifying the Primal Matter within me into Disunification Cosmology.

My work reflects my remembrance of having personally passed through the Disunification of Energy and Awareness.

I was there and so were you.

You can remember it any time you want.

One final note for this chapter: Remembering that you passed through the Disunification does not make you God; the Disunification was a collective experience in which the One became the many.

As will be seen, we are One at the level of Infinity. However, we are not one at the level of the Universe. Knowing this can clear up a great deal of confusion, Pollyannaism, and Utopianism.

Chapter Four

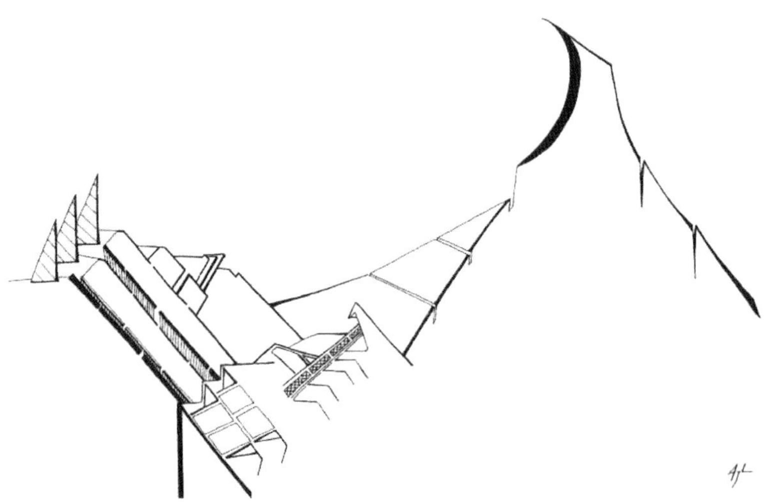

Temple of the Moon

J. Augustine

THE STUNNING SECRETS OF INFINITY

In Infinity, everything exists simultaneously in Unity.

Because Infinity is a Unity, no separate thing can exist therein.

There is no distinction between the personal and the transpersonal, light and darkness, or an idea and its expression. There is only Unity and no separate thing can stand out over or against Unity.

LELA thus suffers the stunning, paradoxical limitation of Infinity: There can be no Creation within Infinity since it must remain an undifferentiated-monolithic Unity.

God has been spoken of as a consuming fire; it has also been said that one cannot look at God and live. And so it is: In the presence of the Infinite One, there is no disunity, no separate thing or self.

Like a great black hole that pulls in every separate thing and reduces it to zero volume, so Infinity reduces any individuality or separateness to zero. None of us could behold the Infinite One and continue to exist as a separate being, for in the presence of totality there is no other. In the moment you or I beheld Infinity, we would no longer have any need for our sub-infinite selves.[3]

Separate selves and individual things could not survive Infinity, for the radioactive presence and psychic onslaught of LELA would annihilate even the mightiest of avatars and the largest of galaxies.

There are no separate selves in Infinity. There are only separate selves in sub-infinite universes, and, all of these separate selves are completely necessary in the scheme of things.

You are necessary in the vast scheme of things.

That you are necessary does not mean you are exempt or immune from anything high or low in the vast range of possibilities.

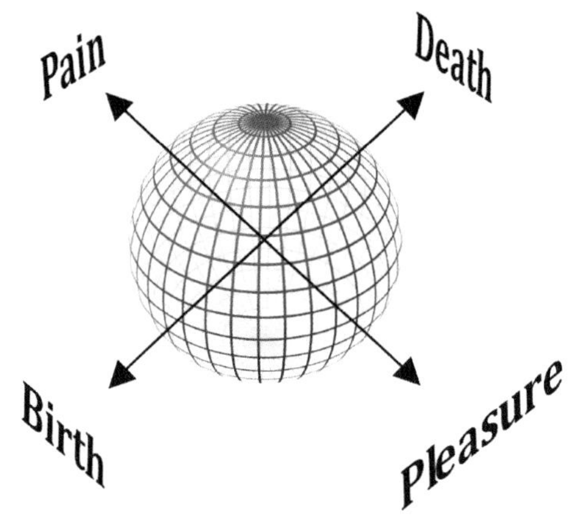

Birth and death – as well as pleasure and pain – are but two examples of the striking and often tortured contrasts inherent in the human condition.

---

[3] For spiritually inclined readers, Appendices A and B contain a more formal spiritual description of LELA.

THE MULTIVERSE

Disunification is inevitable and allows for all universes, all beings, and all of their possible histories to arise.

Infinity is free to spawn:

- ❖ Every possible version and history of our Universe
- ❖ Every possible version of you
- ❖ Every possible version and history of all other universes

Consciousness is intrinsic to the Multiverse.

While Consciousness is entangled in biology, it is not merely, or only, a phenomenon of biology.

Day Teaching is not interested in what has become Materialistic Brain Religion. We embrace Science while rejecting the doctrines of Scientism and Materialism. Moreover, we redefine Spirituality altogether in terms of Consciousness.

Science and Spirituality are both expressions of the vast Spectrum of Consciousness. In terms of Consciousness, then, it is clear that Objectivity and Subjectivity come into play in any discussion of Science and Spirituality.

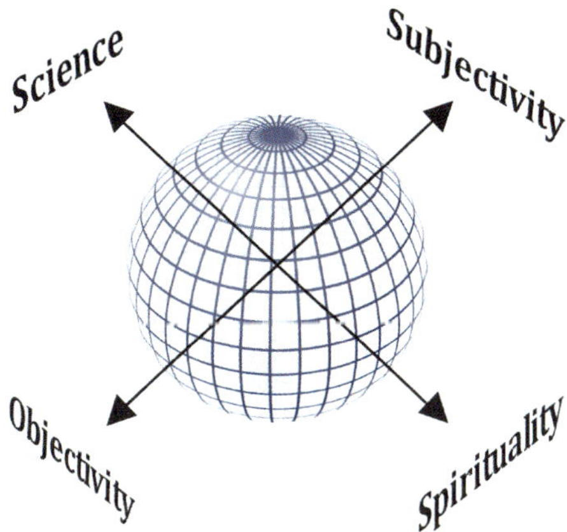

Based on the previous diagram, there are two logical relationships in the Spectrum of Consciousness:

- ❖ **Science and Objectivity**

- ❖ **Spirituality and Subjectivity**

By understanding the Spectrum of Consciousness that came into existence as a function of Disunification, we can begin to place things in proper perspective.

For example, while certain forms of Spirituality can be extraordinarily powerful and useful on a subjective and personal basis, no form of Spirituality can be scientific.

To argue that any form of philosophy or spirituality is "scientific" is utterly absurd. While philosophy or spirituality can be objective in terms of logic and reasoning, neither of them is scientific.

The power of Science is located in its objectivity. Conversely, scientific objectivity goes out the window when scientists make subjective statements about philosophical and spiritual matters. Richard Dawkins castigates religion, but his statements reflect his subjective moral outrage at the abuses of religion.

Scientists making pronouncements about philosophical and spiritual matters are doing so from their own subjective perspective. This is "scientism" which is defined as scientists making subjective ideological pronouncements cloaked in the authority of Science.

In **_The Grand Design,_**[4] a book co-authored by Steven Hawking and Leonard Mlodinow, the two physicists make the pronouncement that philosophy is dead. This is an example of scientists making a subjective ideological statement cloaked in the authority of physics. There is nothing whatsoever objective or scientifically verifiable about such a statement.

---

[4] Stephen Hawking and Leonard Mlodinow, The Grand Design, Bantam Books, 2011.

There is no way to design an experiment that could verify or falsify the claim that philosophy is dead. Hawking and Mlodinow are certainly entitled to their shared opinion about philosophy, but this particular opinion is not even remotely scientific in any way whatsoever, because philosophy and science are at different ends of the Spectrum of Consciousness.

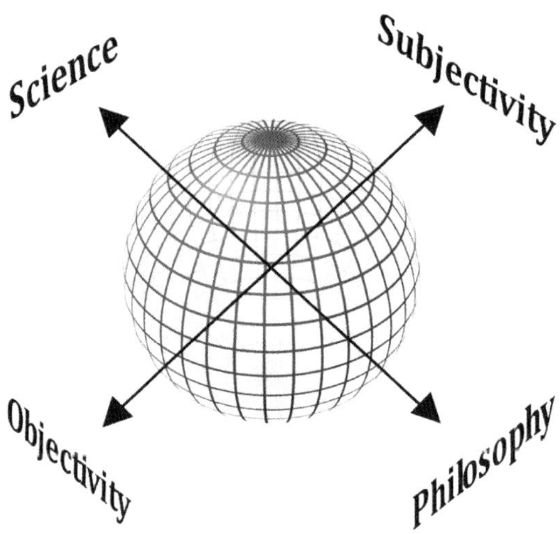

Where exactly on the spectrum Philosophy blends into Science is hard to say. Perhaps it occurs in the new field of study called the Philosophy of Cosmology.

I think it occurs at the Intersection of Disunification, a place located at the corner of Everything and Nothing.

Chapter Five

Sandro Botticelli, The Birth of Venus, circa 1485

The Uffizi Gallery, Florence, Italy

THE DREAMS OF GOD

The notion that God dreams defies the chattering-mind religions of sub-infinite monotheism that deny their Gods any sleep, dreams, mystery, or even oblivion.

Yet, to be truly infinite, God would have to know sleep, dreams, mystery, oblivion, and even what it is like to not be God.

LELA dreams and her dreams become universes in the Multiverse so that she may know and experience all possible states – and this includes you and your own life down to its very last detail.

LELA dreams a special class of dreams called **Day Dreams.**

LELA's Day Dreams serve as the mechanism whereby some part of Infinity is disunified and becomes sub-Infinite universes.

To say that God dreams is anthropomorphic. However, as we can easily identify with dreams, dreaming becomes the most poetic and passionate way we have to describe the Disunification

In any case, the mystics and sages have always told us that we are "arising" in a Great Dream of God and do not realize it.

DISUNIFICATION ONTOLOGY

Before exploring the Dreams of LELA, one particular question must be considered:

How can LELA "dream" and yet still remain "conscious" as God, as the Unity of Infinity?

This question goes to the very core of **Disunification Ontology**.

Wikipedia provides a concise definition of the term Ontology:

"Ontology is the philosophical study of the nature of being, becoming, existence, or reality, as well as the basic categories of being and their relations. Traditionally listed as a part of the major branch of philosophy known as metaphysics, ontology deals with questions concerning what entities exist or can be said to exist, and how such entities can be grouped, related within a hierarchy, and subdivided according to similarities and differences."

Day Teaching is a unique Cosmology embodying an equally unique Ontology.

Philosophically speaking, Disunification is an **ontological transfer mechanism** utilized by Monolithic Infinity.

Disunification is a reduction of Infinity into sub-Infinite forms, processes, and beings intended for transmission into sub-Infinite universes.

Disunification is the mechanism whereby Infinity populates the Multiverse.

Infinity is the ontological existence-granting Source for our Universe and all forms, processes, and beings therein.

In philosophical terms, Disunification negates both Divine Creation and the notion of the Demiurge.

Disunification is necessary for the Multiverse to exist because the direct observation of any sub-Infinite universe by Infinity would instantaneously annihilate that universe.

By analogy, when you begin to awaken from sleep, any dream you were having is annihilated. Your waking self destroys dreams whereas your "dream self" both permits and observes.

Therefore, we use two names for LELA to denote the reduction of the Infinite Source Consciousness.

<u>LELA the Awakened One</u> is the Infinite One who is "awake outside of the Dream" that will become our Universe. The short form of her name is **LELA TAO** and alludes to the *Tao Te Ching.*

<u>LELA the Dreamer</u> is a reduction of the Infinite Source Consciousness into a dreamlike state which permits Disunification to occur.

Essentially, LELA the Dreamer can observe our Universe without annihilating it while LELA TAO remains "awake" as the Infinite One.

LELA the Dreamer is discussed in more detail in chapter twelve.

LELA's Day Dreams are particular types of motions within the Infinite Consciousness in which all kinds of states and conditions can arise that are disallowed in Unity.

The reality you experience when you are awake is quite different than the reality you experience in dreams.

Your dreams are a particular type of motion within your own Consciousness in which all kinds of things can arise that are disallowed within your waking reality.

LELA's dreams last for tens of billions of years whereas your dreams last only for a night.

Nevertheless, your dreams are important events in which your Soul disunifies some symbolic part of itself in order to explore, understand, or express that which it cannot fully comprehend, acknowledge, or permit in the waking state.

While this book is not a study about dream language and symbols, there is no doubt about the importance of dreams and learning the dream language of your Soul.

MYSTERY LAND

Where do LELA's dreams occur?

LELA's Dreams originate in the *Mystery Land*.

Mystery exists within Infinity because Infinity contains all things, including mystery, paradoxes, and contradictions.

Mystery Land is a transitional boundary region between Infinity and the Multiverse that speaks to the Hartle-Hawking State:

> "In theoretical physics, the Hartle–Hawking state, named after James Hartle and Stephen Hawking, is a proposal concerning the state of the universe prior to the Planck epoch. Hartle-Hawking is essentially a no-boundary proposal that the universe is infinitely finite: that there was no time before the Big Bang because time did not exist before the formation of spacetime associated with the Big Bang and subsequent expansion of the universe in space and time.[5]"

Time and space are bound in Infinity and so neither is expressed therein.

There is no boundary to our universe because time and space end at its boundary. It is meaningless to speak of boundaries where time and space do not exist.

As a consequence of Disunification, our sub-Infinite Universe can only be "infinitely finite."

In my view, Disunification does not technically violate the Hartle-Hawking State. As I later contend, on this side of things our Universe could indeed look like it spontaneously appeared out of nowhere.

Mystery Land is the transitional region in which the jump from Infinity to sub-infinity occurs.

---

[5] Wikipedia: http://en.wikipedia.org/wiki/Hartle%E2%80%93Hawking_state

THE UNCREATE

Mystery Land speaks to the **Uncreate** aspect of Infinity.

The Uncreate is Infinity that has not yet been disunified into Primal Matter in order to source a universe.

Mystery Land is the region in Infinity wherein some small part of Infinity is "harvested" so that it can be disunified into Primal Matter.

What exists in the Primal Matter is a Mystery to Infinity. Thus, LELA TAO must disunify the Primal Matter in order to discover who and what exists within.

The Mystery inherent in Infinity can only be accessed within the sub-infinite universes, called the **Lower Worlds**.

The inherent potential in the Primal Matter is fully disunified, evolved, and realized over eons of time and universes.

Stated another way, God evolves via the process of **Disunification-Evolution** within the Lower Worlds. We discuss Disunification-Evolution in chapter seventeen.

PREEXISTENT PRIMAL MATTER

Day Teaching inherently maintains that the sum total of everything in our Universe preexisted within Infinity prior to our Universe.

Judeo-Christianity asserts that matter did not exist prior to our Universe. This is a very important point because Judeo-Christianity declares that God "spoke" our physical Universe into existence.

Judeo-Christianity cannot allow for preexistent matter as this would mean that its God did not create the universe but rather fashioned it from preexistent matter. This implies that preexistent matter would be equal to and thus co-eternal with God.

This is simply not allowable in biblical thinking.

In Judeo-Christian thinking, nothing can be greater than the Bible God, particularly something as ordinary as Matter. In the Book of Genesis, then, the God of the Bible "spoke" the Universe into existence from nothing, i.e. there was no preexistent matter.

St. Augustine of Hippo used the Latin term **Creation Ex Nihilo**, which means **Creation from Nothing**.

The upshot of Biblical Creation is that the entire human race is morally accountable to the God of the Bible.

More precisely, the human race is morally accountable to whatever Church, Pope, or President speaks on behalf of the God of the Bible.

Divine Creation is untrue and has always been a tool used to control the religious masses whose identities depend upon their belief in a Creator-God.

Divine Creation is not needed to explain the appearance of our Universe or the fact of Consciousness.

We affirm Consciousness itself while throwing out the stagnant old Creationist bathwater in which both Christian and Islamic violence grows.

Matter is preexistent. To be specific, all of the Matter in our Universe preexisted as the unified Life Energy and Life Awareness of Infinity.

Disunification occurred as a result of both Something and Nothing.

The Something was the Primal Matter.

The Nothing was Nothing.

PERFECTION VS. DISUNIFICATION

Monotheistic theologians insist that their God is holy, sinless, perfect, and complete.

They cannot allow their God to evolve, for this would require an admission that their God is not perfect and complete.

God's perfection in turn drives the demand that believers seek to attain God's holiness, sinlessness, perfection, and completion.

This is simply impossible given the fact that human Consciousness is derived from Infinity.

We each contain a vast expanse that includes Good and Evil.

Thus, conventional monotheistic religion and its expectations for perfection are abandoned.

Unrealistic moral standards breed hypocrisy.

In place of an unattainable and unnecessary holiness, we invoke Karma, the inexorable law that one reaps what one sows.

There are very real consequences for one's own actions in our disunified Universe.

It is both meaningless and unnecessary to speak of LELA TAO as being holy, sinless, perfect, and complete.

That paradigm is purely monotheistic and unrealistic.

For that reason, LELA TAO is spoken of as a Monolithic Unity.

Thus:

❖ LELA TAO desires to disunify and explore the Uncreate in the Lower Worlds.

❖ The Lower Worlds are the Uncreate disunified and made available for existential exploration, evolution, experimentation, art, and all other avenues whereby all forms of knowledge and experience may be acquired.

Disunification allows LELA TAO to take some new fraction of the Uncreate apart, so that she can experience herself not as Infinity, but rather from the point of view of sub-infinite beings, such as you and me.

We are not God – We are God disunified.

Having at one time been Infinite, you can innately remember what it was like to be God.

This is why you are frustrated that you are not God.

This is the frustration of limitation that comes with Disunification.

Therefore, into the Lower Worlds we must go.

There was no Fall; there was Good and Evil disunifying into human Consciousness.

We no longer need the Garden of Eden to explain Good and Evil when we understand Disunification.

Come with me and remember Infinity and the Disunification.

We now proceed now into **Mystery-Land** where LELA's Day dreams take place.

SECTION II

HARVESTING THE PRIMAL MATTER

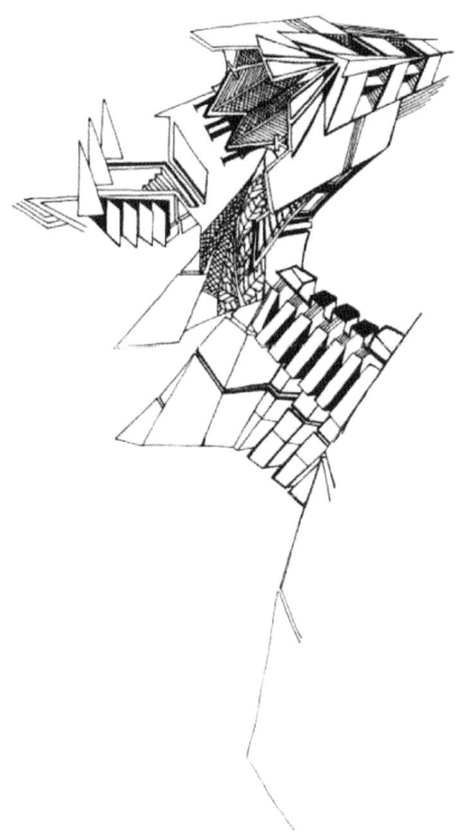

Primal Matter Disunifying from Infinity

J. Augustine

Chapter Six

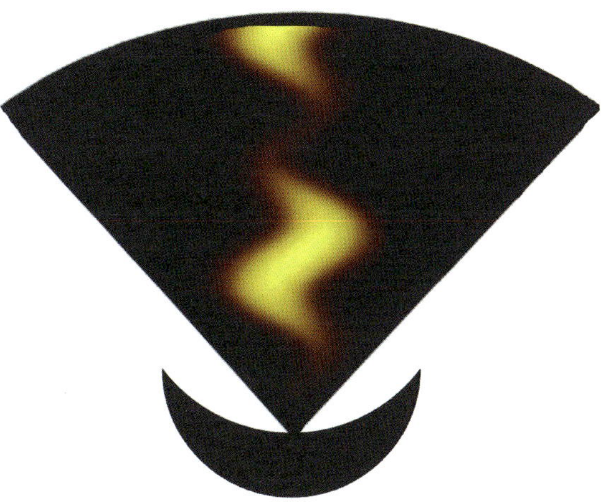

The Psycho-Active Ark of the Dream Tribe

J. Augustine, 2007

LELA'S DREAM TRIBES

It is axiomatic in Day Teaching that Infinity is one thing that can disunify itself into all things. Hence, Infinity is one thing that becomes two things, and then three things, and then all things. Disunification is the way in which the One becomes the Many.

Dreaming is a metaphor for the way in which Disunification begins in Infinity. It is like this in your own dreams, in which all sorts of separate people, places, and events occur.

You are the "Source Consciousness" from which all of these separate people, places, and events arise. In the same way, LELA TAO is the "Source Consciousness" from which her Dream Tribes arise and harvest the Primal Matter that will become everything in our Universe, including you and me.

LELA's dreams are motions in the Infinite Consciousness that we personify in a story about her Dream Tribes. This story is told as a Mystery Play, a public telling of what caused the Big Bang. In this play, the actors are LELA's Dream Tribes.

THE DREAM TRIBES ARISE

LELA the Dreamer and her Dream Tribe as symbolized by the use of an ancient Hindu sculpture.

This sculpture shows the Goddess asleep on her couch while being attended to by her servants.

The Dream Tribes are *Agents of Disunification*.

They arise as a function of Disunification for the sole purpose of Disunification.

The Dream Tribes do not create on behalf of LELA TAO. Rather, they disunify Infinity as an autonomous collective dedicated to reproducing an exact and faithful reproduction of LELA's Dream of our Universe.

THE CONCEPT OF THE DEMIURGE

Disunification Cosmology does not employ the ancient religious concept of a ***Demiurge***.

For readers unfamiliar with the term "Demiurge," below are definitions from two sources. The first is from gnosis.org:

> Valentinus founded a school of speculative Christian theology in the second century AD. Because he and his followers drew a distinction between the true God and the creator of the world, they are classified by modern scholars as 'Gnostics.' In common with other Gnostics, they believed that the material world was created by a lesser deity which they call the Demiurge (literally 'public craftsman').[6]

The second definition is from *New Advent*, an excellent online Catholic encyclopedia. As such, it is a Catholic definition and thus views the term "Demiurge" from a wholly Christian perspective:

> ***Demiurge:*** The word means literally a public worker, demioergós, demiourgós, and was originally used to designate any craftsman plying his craft or trade for the use of the public. Soon, however, technites and other words began to be used to designate the common artisan while demiurge was set aside for the Great Artificer or Fabricator, the Architect of the universe. At first the words toû kósmou were added to distinguish the great Workman from others, but gradually demiourgós became the technical term for the Maker of heaven and earth. In this sense it is used frequently by Plato in his 'Timæus.' Although often loosely employed by the Fathers and others to indicate the Creator, the word never strictly meant "one who produces out of nothing" (for this the Greeks used ktístes), but only "one who fashions, shapes, and models." A creator in the sense of Christian theology

---

[6] Retrieved online at: http://www.gnosis.org/library/valentinus/Demiurge.htm

has no place in heathen philosophy, which always presupposes the existence of matter. Moreover, according to Greek philosophy the world-maker is not necessarily identical with God, as first and supreme source of all things; he may be distinct from and inferior to the supreme spirit, though he may also be the practical expression of the reason of God, the Logos as operative in the harmony of the universe. In this sense, i.e. that of a world-maker distinct from the Supreme God, Demiurge became a common term in Gnosticism."[7]

Note the statement in the Catholic definition: "A creator in the sense of Christian theology has no place in heathen philosophy, which always presupposes the existence of matter."

In ancient pre-Christian thinking, the Demiurge was conceived of as a spiritual agency or a spiritual being who created the Universe out of preexistent matter on behalf of God.

This begs the question of why a monotheistic God would have some other party create our Universe.

At the risk of oversimplification, certain pre-Christian philosophers and later groups, such as the Gnostics, believed that a pure Spirit-God would not contaminate himself in Matter.

Therefore, God outsourced the creation of the Universe to a "world-maker" called a Demiurge.

The Demiurge is said to have fashioned preexistent Chaos – or some form of preexistent, primordial, uncreated matter – into our Universe. For this reason, a Demiurge-fashioned Universe is seen as flawed and corrupt because it does not perfectly express God, who is assumed to be perfect.

---

[7] Retrieved online at: http://www.newadvent.org/cathen/04707b.htm

The Demiurge is conceived of as being lower in power and ability than God. Hence, the Demiurge was unable to filter out, purify, or otherwise tame the imperfections, passions, violence, and lusts inherent into the preexistent Chaos.

As a result, these imperfections were transmitted into our Universe and into the Gods, Goddesses, angels, demons, humans and everything else.

It follows, then, that humans must engage in a lifetime, or lifetimes, of spiritual purification in order to attain the purity of God.

THE REJECTION OF THE DEMIURGE

Due to the Creation narrative offered in the Book of Genesis, Judeo-Christianity and Islam have always rejected the notion of a Demiurge.

The concept of a Demiurge is an insult to Creator-God religions.

The central argument of monotheists is that their God spoke our Universe into existence and that there was absolutely no preexistent matter or anything else.

Day Teaching does not argue for Divine Creation, a Demiurge, or an inexplicable Big Bang, but rather that our Universe was disunified from Infinity.

LELA's Dream Tribe does one thing and that is to disunify some part of Infinity. To "disunify Infinity" is radically different than the three current paradigms:

❖ Divine Creation

❖ The Demiurge creating the Universe out of preexistent matter. The Dream Tribe arises in Infinity as a motion within Infinity and is not demiurgical in nature

❖ A spontaneous Big Bang in which our physical Universe appeared due to some sort of hypothetical disturbance

The Mystery Play about to be enacted answers the two basic questions posed at the beginning of the book:

Where did the Black Pearl that exploded into our Universe come from?

The answer is that the Black Pearl originated in Infinity as a virtual object called a ***Day Sphere.***

We represent a Day Sphere using the simple image of a sphere.

Mystery Land is shot through with Day Spheres of all sizes into which small parts of Infinity may be disunified.

The spheres, or bubbles, serve an illustrative purpose only. They are not a statement on the shape of our Universe or of any other universe.

All of these empty Day Spheres can be populated with different combinations of Primal Matter.

Thus, there are limitless types of different universes in the Multiverse.

Each possible universe is constrained based upon a set of codes unique to that Universe.

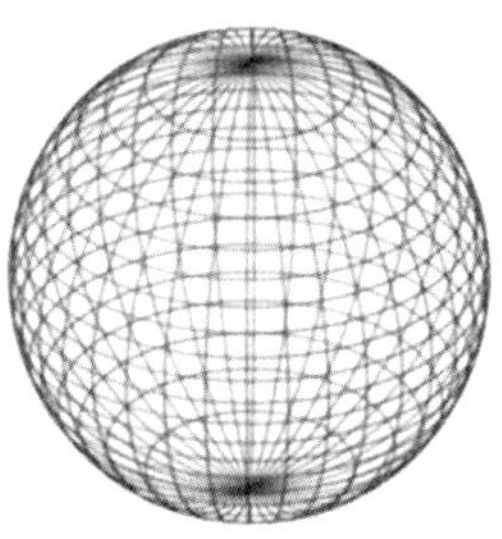

Nothing is located within a Day Sphere.

The coding is done as a function of Disunification.

The second question:

How did all of the Primal Matter get packaged into the tiny Black Pearl in the first place?

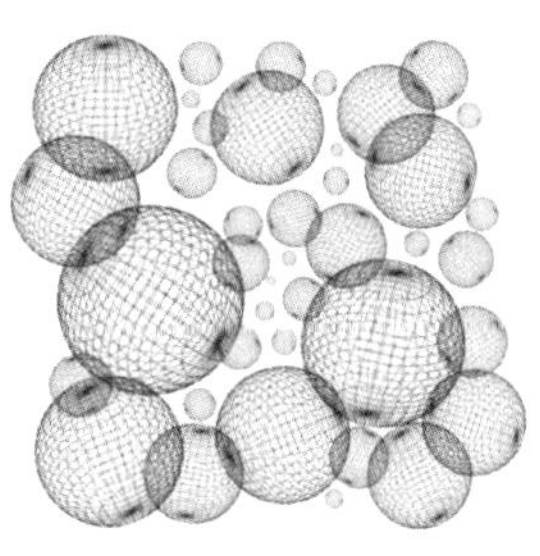

As described in the next several chapters, LELA's Dream Tribe harvested the Primal Matter from Infinity and then stored it in the Day Sphere that was to become our Universe.

The process of Disunification then compressed both the Day Sphere and the Primal Matter into a **Black Pearl** singularity.

This singularity instantaneously and massively disunified into our Universe.

On this side of things – in our Universe – the Disunification Event looked like an uncaused and unexplainable Big Bang.

Chapter Seven

Tropical Storm with Tiger, Henri Rousseau, 1891

BULDING A DAY DREAM

Gathering from among their dwelling places in the majestic, beautiful, and faraway Dream Sanctuaries of Mystery Land, LELA's Dream Tribe secretly assembles in the Jungle where the Dreaming Pool is hidden.

The countless faces of the Dream Tribe gather round the Dreaming Pool and peer into its shimmering infinite Void.

From the formlessness of the Void emerge lovely geishas walking in bamboo and tall grass. Streaky dragons spiral out of the mists and, as they do, they whirl and spin ever higher above the Dreaming Pool. The dragons' great gravity sweeps the geishas up to the Heavens. Dragons and geishas are transformed into spiraling zodiacs of synaptic-superclusters that stream Zen music.

The lovely Geishas reappear on high and ride the streaky-zodiac dragons far beyond the Sky, disappearing in the direction of their distant, faraway, future incarnations.

Torrents of images, a cacophony of sound, blazing blue seraphim-pumped lasers, the alchemy of blood, flesh, and bone, of abstract codes of gravity and antigravity continue in a procession that now jumps up from the depths of the Dreaming Pool.

This majestic procession breathtakingly transforms itself into a dazzling, jeweled Phalanx of Storks that takes flight across the endless Blue Jungle Sky. The Phalanx of jeweled Storks ascends and disappears into the Blinding Lights of Endless Desire.

Far off in the distance, a multitude of dreamed-of-people wonder with fascination toward perfectly white windmills scattered across wheat fields on this Horizon of Perfection.

The beguiling Horizon of Perfection stretches out as if it were endless, but then it turns and surreptitiously drops off into stony sharp-rock canyons filled with ancient gnarled trees that kiss the new thundercloud skies of an imagined day in a great canyon system.

The wanderers stop on their way to the perfectly white windmills and turn their heads towards the Blinding Lights of Endless Desires to look at the returning Storks.

The Phalanx of jeweled Storks suddenly descend from on high and explode into a pristine, crystalline meteor shower of fiery luminescent diamonds, rubies, sapphires, and other precious stones that rain down upon the Jungle.

The Dream Tribe catches these blazing stones in baskets woven of crimson and blue.

The Dream Tribe looks into the fiery stones and becomes transfixed by the Day Dream encoded within and its visions of a dazzlingly starry, far-off place.

The beauty of this place strikes them as being so utterly essential that they vow to bring this dream into reality.

The Dream Tribe surrenders to the beauty of LELA's Desire and vows to give her yet another Jewel Box universe laden with diamonds, physics, necklaces, fine wine, charmed quarks, exotic islands in the sea, and all other natural luxuries.

Nothing will be held back; LELA will have her Desire.

Suddenly, the dreamed-of-people are now gone, for the first part of the Day Dream is over. The lush, fertile Jungle of Primordial Chaos is quiet once again.

Not all of the Dream Tribe wants to be disunified, but these purists are nevertheless swept away in the Great Motion of Desire.

Against their will, these members of the Dream Tribe will be pulled down into the Lower Worlds where they will be disunified, evolved, and expanded out into an incalculable Void.

The Void and Disunification terrifies those who desire to remain One in Infinity. Yet, the Motion is carried.

The seduction and adventure of the Lower Worlds is so great that it overtakes even the Renunciates.

THE NINE DREAM TRIBES

The Dream Tribe divides itself into nine smaller tribes.

Each of these smaller tribes has a specialty that will be needed to transform the Dream into our Universe.

The division of labor agreed upon, the nine tribes split up and head off into the Dream Sanctuaries to undertake their respective tasks of harvesting the Primal Matter.

Below are the functions LELA's nine Dream Tribes will perform in the pre-Universe of Mystery Land:

- Dream Tribe I: The Dream Tribe Masons

- Dream Tribe II: The Fundamental Forces

- Dream Tribes III: Particles and Wavelengths

- Dream Tribes IV & V: The Programmers of the Source Codes

- Dream Tribe VI: Communications and Interfaces

- Dream Tribe VI: The Hall of Records

- Dream Tribe VII: Embodying the Dreamer

- Dream Tribes VIII & IX: Initiating the Disunification

The Primal Matter harvested from Infinity will be taken and assembled inside of the particular Day Sphere that will become our Universe.

Chapter Eight

The Giza Complex

DREAM TRIBE I:

QUARRYING INFINITY

Analogies are presented to help visualize the process of Disunification.

The first analogy is to the Great Pyramid of Giza. This Great Pyramid is a classic symbol of mystery and antiquity whose construction is a mystery, for no one really knows how it was made.

The Great Pyramid represents unparalleled skill. The precision of its construction and its geographical alignment relative to the Heavens and Earth mark it as the unique building on our planet.

Together with its leonine companion The Sphinx, the Great Pyramid has yet to give up all of its secrets.

The duty of the stonemasons in ages past here on Earth was to quarry, shape, and fit stones artfully together into majestic buildings such as the Great Pyramid. Stone edifices erected by masons have lasted for millennia due to the quality of the building materials and workmanship. Masons built the Giza complex with its three perfect, and perfectly aligned, stone pyramids.

The Duty of the Dream Tribe Masons is to quarry certain stones from Infinity and then build them into a faster-than-light virtual machine. This machine will be used to transport the Primal Matter out of Infinity.

MAX PLANCK

The second analogy is to the work of Max Planck (1858 – 1947), who originated quantum theory. At the beginning of the twentieth century, Planck studied the way in which heat was emitted and absorbed by metal. Among his other discoveries, Planck's studies led him to observe that energy is always emitted or absorbed in "packets" which Planck called "quanta."

Planck's breakthrough discovery was that energy propagates, or travels, in discrete packets. Planck's work allowed physicists to conceptualize energy in terms of packets, or quanta, which in turn led to a new understanding of subatomic particles.

Just as science had discovered that matter was made of atoms, Planck discovered that energy existed in the form of quanta and this had major implications for modern physics.

The analogy to Planck reveals that the Primal Matter of our Universe was quantized in the Disunification. Energy can only exist in our Universe as packets; therefore it was disunified in packet form.

Things can only be transported out of Infinity in packets. Thus, the Dream Tribes work to quantize some small part of Infinity.

DREAM TRIBE I

Because our Universe will be physical and must last tens of billions of years or more, the Dream Tribe I are Masons who will quarry the indestructible stone of Life Energy.

When disunified, the Life Energy becomes physical Energy that can neither be created nor destroyed. Furthermore, as Einstein taught us, Energy and Mass are convertible: $E=MC^2$.

Because Consciousness will be intrinsic in our Universe and must exist for tens of billions of years or more, the Dream Tribe Masons also quarry the indestructible stone of Life Awareness.

When disunified, the Life Awareness becomes Consciousness that can neither be created nor destroyed. The Life Awareness will be disunified into all forms of disunified Consciousness including:

❖ The Spectrum of Consciousness

❖ The Unconsciousness

❖ Archetypes

❖ Karma

❖ All sentient beings in our Universe

Having quarried these special stones, the Dream Tribe Masons fit them carefully into the empty "main body" of the Day Dream Pyramid.

The main body of the Day Dream Pyramid in a 3/4 view. The top stone – or pyramidion – has not yet been placed atop the pyramid.

Chapter Nine

Jacob's Ladder, circa 1800
William Blake

DREAM TRIBE II:

THE FUNDAMENTAL FORCES

Descending into an Abyss in Infinity, Dream Tribe II locates the fundamental forces required to impose structure on the new Universe when it is booted up at superluminal speed in the Disunification.

The fundamental forces are seamlessly unified into Infinity. Dream Tribe II must therefore perform three basic functions:

1. Harvest, or disunify, the fundamental forces from Infinity. The fundamental forces are gravity; electromagnetism; the strong force; and the weak force.

2. Package the fundamental forces into the body of the Day Dream Pyramid.

3. Ensure that the fundamental forces will be disunified in an exact matter when the Disunification occurs.

THE DOUBLE HELIX TOWER

After harvesting the fundamental forces from Infinity, Dream Tribe II assembles them into a Double Helix Tower placed in the vertical centerline of the Pyramid:

The Double Helix Tower symbolizes the stored, coiled energy of the fundamental forces awaiting Disunification.

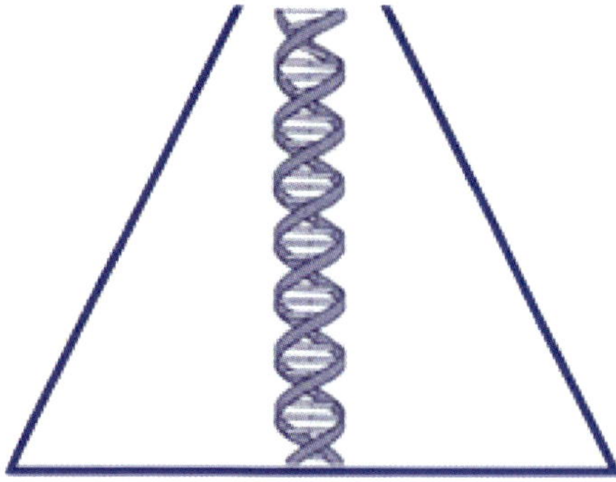

The sudden release of the stored energy in the fundamental forces will contribute extreme speed and power to the Disunification.

The shape of the Double Helix Tower as DNA alludes to order.

Indeed, the placement of all subsequent items into the main body of the Pyramid is done in a particular order. This placement allows for a specific unpackaging sequence to occur when the Disunification occurs.

Our Universe must be unpackaged in a very specific sequence, and under specific conditions of speed and heat, in order for it to appear.

Chapter Ten

Image: NASA[8]

DREAM TRIBE III:

PARTICLES AND WAVELENGTHS

Following the completion of its work on the main body of the Pyramid, Dream Tribe III harvests the Primal Matter that will become the Electromagnetic Spectrum of our Universe:

---

[8] From NASA: "Artist's concept of the star Fomalhaut and the Jupiter-type planet that the Hubble Space Telescope observed. A ring of debris appears to surround Fomalhaut as well. The planet, called Fomalhaut b, orbits the 200-million-year-old star every 872 years." Credit: ESA, NASA, and L. Calcada (ESO for STScI)" Retrieved online at:
http://www.nasa.gov/mission_pages/hubble/science/fomalhaut.html

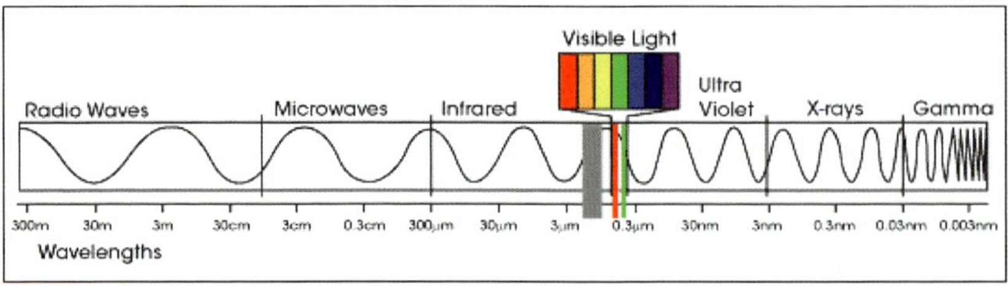

The Dream Tribe works to ensure that the electromagnetic spectrum will propagate as an exact and faithful reproduction of LELA's Day Dream of our Universe.

When Dream Tribe III affixes these radiant jewels to the tower, it becomes the *Jeweled Tower*.

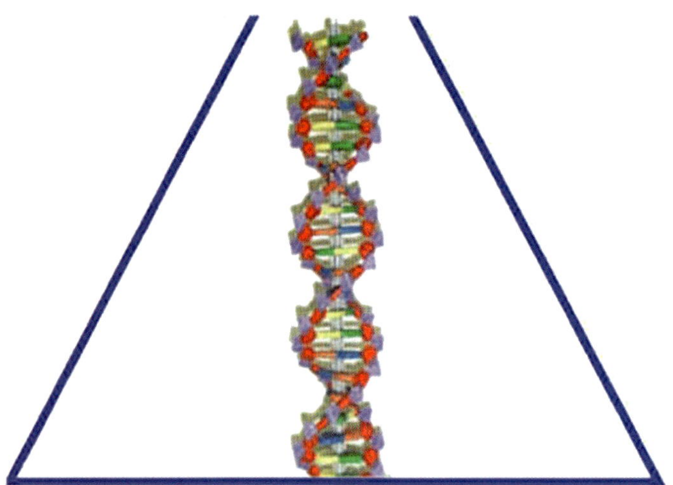

**The Electromagnetic Spectrum is wrapped
around the Double Helix Tower.**

Chapter Eleven

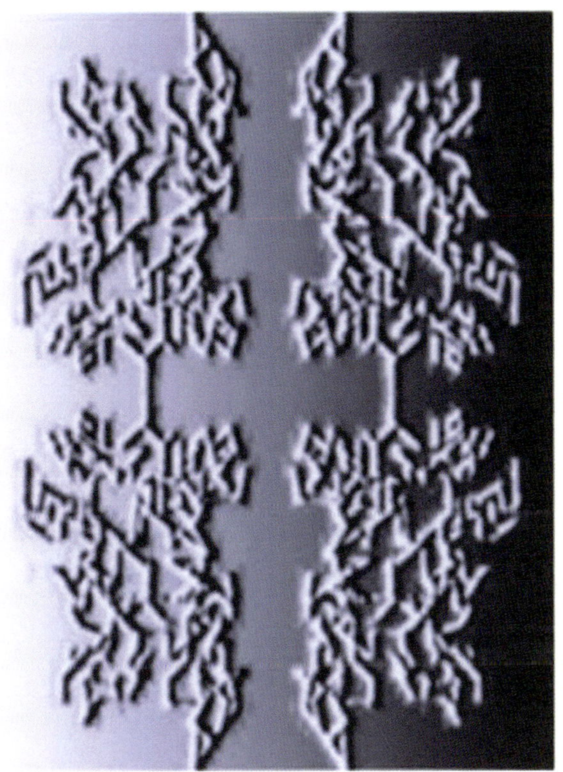

The Source Codes

DREAM TRIBES IV & V:

THE SOURCE CODES

Because the Disunification happens so quickly, it will be initiated and controlled by highly automated programs.

Automation will be true of much of our Universe and everything therein. This automation requires that instructions – in the form of the Source Codes of Disunification – be written by the "Programming Dream Tribes" IV and V.

The Source Codes are symbolized by the image that opens this chapter. The image depicts the Source Codes as strings etched onto a gray-blue substrate.

This symbol abstractly refers to "strings and source codes" being harvested from Infinity and then "vacuum-welded" into the very fabric our Universe. Hence, the structure and physical laws of our Universe are immutable.

PLATO'S FORMS

To this point, the Dream Tribe's translation of LELA TAO's Vision into our finite universe speaks to Plato's notions of Forms. However, it is more complex than Plato's Forms.

There is no perfect idea in the mind of God. There is rather every possibility and every history of any given Form. The necessity for the Multiverse arises so that everything in Infinity can ultimately be disunified, evolved, and realized.

If you prefer classical terms, this is "God's Will" for both our Universe and each of us. We will be fully disunified, evolved, and unfolded over time. This is inevitable: Infinity will have its way.

At the top level, the purpose of our Universe – and of all sentient beings – is to unpackage and evolve the very Primal Matter of Infinity. This abstract purpose becomes very personal to each of us as we must incarnate and live it. There is inherent existential tension in Disunification.

The Mystery is not about God. The Mystery is about what is inside of the Primal Matter and how to best disunify, evolve, and optimize it.

We came from Infinity in our primal form and we will return to Infinity in our evolved and optimized form. The Source Codes of Disunification will inexorably act to ensure that optimization occurs across the billions of years that our Universe will exist.

THE ARCANE PANDECT OF

LELA'S DREAM

The Dream Tribe Programmers labor deep in the Heart of the Day Dream.

There, they translate the arcane pandect of LELA's Dream into the complex codes by which our new Universe will unfold, evolve, and operate.

These programs are known as the **Source Codes of Disunification** (SCD's).

The SCD's ensure that our Universe will be a true and faithful reproduction of LELA's Dream of our Universe.

There is a correspondence between the two, but it is not exact for the simple reason that our Universe is a finite representation of an Infinite Vision.

In this sense, LELA's Vision speaks to the notion of Plato's forms.

The Source Codes of Disunification include instruction sets that will be invoked at the moment of Disunification.

These instruction sets will allow the new Universe to unpackage and sequence itself on an automated basis.

The Source Codes constrain our Universe so that it must be the way it is and cannot be some other way.

Of course, just as human programmers leave clues behind in their games and programs, we would expect that LELA's Dream Tribe left clues behind for us to find. This is why there are Dream Tribe clues scattered all over the Heavens and the Earth, two of which are the Golden Ratio and Fibonacci numbers?

Dream Tribes IV & V integrate the Source Codes into the integrated communications systems and feedback loops of our Universe.

This work speaks to the deeply interconnected nature of our Universe.

Structures ranging from subatomic particles to supercluster galaxies and everything in between are interconnected in ways we do not fully understand at present.

The Dream Tribes work to seamlessly interconnect everything in our Universe.

From the **quantum nonlocality** of physics to the **dependent arising** of Buddhism (pratītyasamutpāda), our Universe will be massively synchronized, interconnected, and networked.

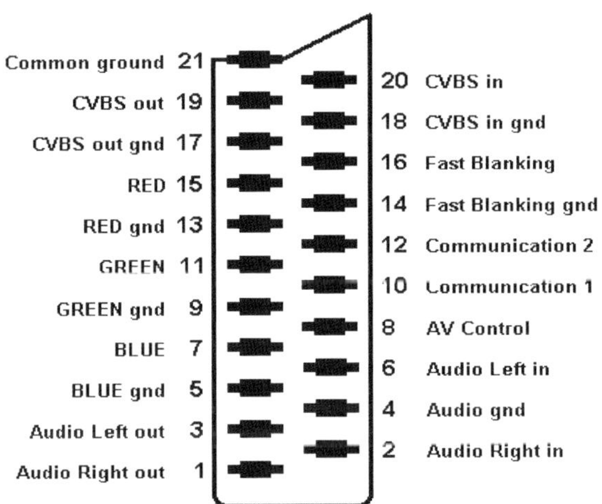

Considering the minimal complexity of the Scart 20-pin Euro connector, we can imagistically scale it up to universal-level to envision the massive interconnectivity of our Universe.

We place the symbol of the Source Codes in the Day Dream Pyramid:

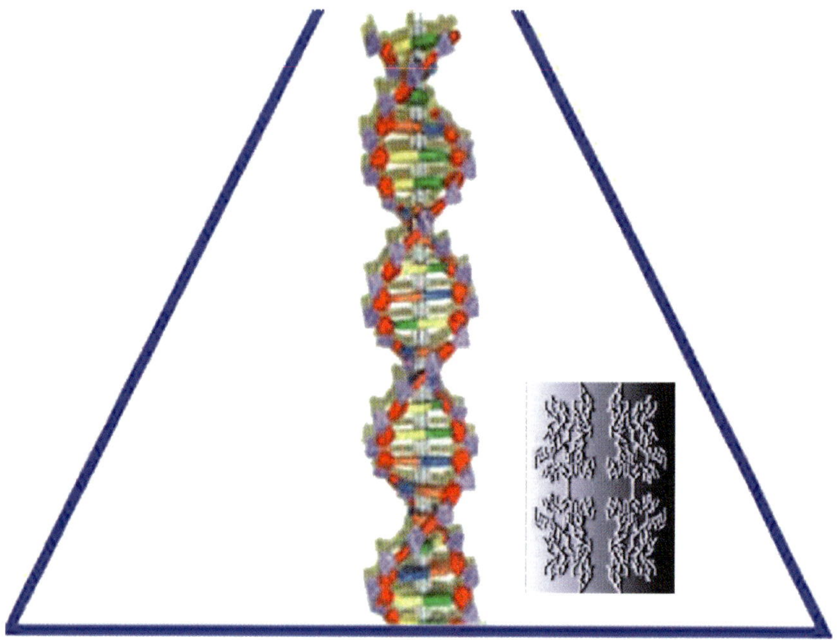

Chapter Twelve

Hermes Trismegistus

DREAM TRIBE VI:

RECORDING THE UNIVERSE

If a tree falls in the forest and no one hears it, does it make a sound?

If a universe exists and no one sees it or experiences it, does it exist?

Day Teaching maintains that there must be at least one Witness, or Observer, if any sub-Infinite universe is to exist.

And as we noted previously, the direct observation of Infinity would annihilate our Universe. Thus, LELA the Dreamer observes our Universe from a sub-Infinite state following the Disunification.

Specifically, the Dreamer observes our Universe as the ontological-existence-granting agent of Infinity.

LELA the Dreamer is the singular high level Witness of our Universe. She is "Eternal in the Heavens" and will live forever, i.e. for the duration of our Universe.

Because she will be disunified as herself from Infinity, it is true to say that LELA the Dreamer was never born and will never die – this relative to our Universe. This condition will also be true of certain other beings that will be disunified. We address this particular class of beings in Section V.

The Dreamer is the one who observes LELA's Day Dream unfold even as we observe our dreams unfold and so give them reality.

In an abstract, phenomenal sense, each of us is granted our basic reality by the peerless gaze of LELA the Dreamer.

For reasons that will be made clear, you do not, and cannot, witness our Universe in the same way as does LELA the Dreamer.

THE PERVASIVE WITNESSING CONSCIOUSNESS

LELA the Dreamer is the *Pervasive Witnessing Consciousness* that observes our entire Universe and thus permits it to exist as a Universe.

In her capacity as the Pervasive Witnessing Consciousness of our Universe, we symbolize the LELA the Dreamer by use of the All Seeing Eye of Antiquity.

The widely known *Eye of Horus* is used to symbolize the Witness function of the Dreamer.

LELA the Dreamer is not a monotheistic tyrant who conducts nonstop surveillance on people in order to judge them.

The function of LELA the Dreamer is to simply be a Witness of the sum total of everything that happens in our Universe.

What does LELA the Dreamer do with everything she observes from the pre-Disunification to the end of our Universe?

Dream Tribes VI ensure that the Dreamer's all-pervasive observational stream is recorded and archived into a Cloud that has near-Infinite storage capacity. Their job is to establish and configure this storage Cloud so that it deploys in the Disunification.

In the first second of Disunification, LELA the Dreamer will record everything she witnessed from the moment she awakened in the Day Dream forward. As previously stated, I remember the pre-Disunification and having passing through the Disunification. As part of my own work, this book is my true and faithful record of what I personally witnessed.

Qabala with Lightning Strike

J. Augustine
Collage of NASA images

THE DREAMER MANDALA

LELA TAO will accept nothing less than a true and faithful record of our Universe.

This true and faithful record is what will be uploaded back into Infinity when our Universe ends.

The need for this record is why a universal storage Cloud with near-Infinite capacity is established by Dream Tribe VI.

In ancient spiritual traditions, the idea of a near-Infinite storage Cloud that records the Universe could not be conceived of as there were no computers or storage clouds.

Rather, the widespread monotheistic belief was that God recorded everything for later use as evidence in the Day of Judgment.

An older esoteric concept maintains that the Cosmic Mandala is a universal "Hall of Records" that contains esoteric knowledge in addition to storing the ongoing record of the Universe.

In Day Teaching, we thematically borrow the older concept of the "Cosmic Mandala" to speak of the near-Infinite storage Cloud utilized by LELA the Dreamer.

We call our recording device the ***Dreamer Mandala.***

We define the Dreamer Mandala as the universally-pervasive storage Cloud embedded into the very fabric and structure of our Universe. The Dreamer Mandala is inherent and will pervade every form, process, and being in our Universe.

LELA the Dreamer is universally co-pervasive with the Mandala. However, LELA the Dreamer is differentiated from the Mandala for two key reasons:

- LELA the Dreamer is a specialized and pristine form of Consciousness.
- The Mandala is a specialized and pristine automated machine network. It is the black box recorder of our Universe.

We symbolize the Dreamer Mandala by placing LELA the Dreamer inside of a triangle where the triangle denotes our Universe. Hence, the Dreamer Mandala pervades our Universe:

The Dreamer Mandala

THE MANDALA OF INFINITY

A related symbol is more elaborate and is entitled ***The Mandala of Infinity***:

The Mandala of Infinity is a composite symbol in which a basic geometric mandala is superimposed on a triangle.

In this symbol, the triangle denotes our Universe and the mandala represents the Unity of Infinity. Hence, our disunified Universe arises within the Unity of Infinity.

THE NECESSITY OF RECORDING

Why is Infinity interested in having our Universe witnessed and recorded down the very last quantum-mechanical detail? Why is LELA the Witness and the Cosmic Mandala needed?

They are needed because LELA TAO spawns universes based upon this principle:

Infinity is content hungry

What Infinity specifically wants is Primal Matter that has been disunified and evolved by streaming through the structures of universes and the lives of sentient beings.

Because she cannot participate in universes from their inceptions through to their collapses, LELA TAO has all universes reunified and uploaded back into Infinity when they are finished.

"God" evolves in and through the countless forms of the Multiverse, and, each of us is a part of the Multiverse.

In our Universe, LELA the Witness and the Cosmic Mandala serve the principle of Infinity to acquire all disunified content.

Nothing and no one has ever been lost. Nothing and no one will ever be lost.

OUR ACQUISITIVE NATURE

Our disunified Universe is inherently acquisitive.

This term "acquisitive" means that our Universe intrinsically records everything always.

This term "acquisitive" also means that our Universe intrinsically acts to unpackage, evolve, and acquire as much content as possible.

Our Universe lasts a long time because that is how long it will take to unpackage and evolve the Primal Matter allotted to us by Infinity.

You are Eternal and will also last for the full extent of our Universe, after which time you will merge back into Infinity.

Day Teaching maintains that humans are acquisitive and thus undergo both rebirth and reincarnation in order to both acquire and exhaust all of their possibilities on the human level[9].

---

[9] The difference between rebirth and reincarnation is explained in chapter twenty-seven.

THE CAPSTONE ON THE PYRAMID

We symbolize LELA the Dreamer and the Cosmic Mandala by combining them into a Pyramidion.

What is a Pyramidion?

It is the capstone that sets atop a completed pyramid.

The capstone for the Day Dream Pyramid is the Dreamer Mandala:

In ancient Egypt, the capstone on a pyramid was called the **Benben**. This name was derived from the original Benben, a sacred pyramidion that was said to have plunged downwards from the heavens to the earth.

The Benben was associated with **Ra-Atum**, the highest God in the Egyptian pantheon. The Ancient Egyptian Pyramid Texts declare of Ra-Atum:

"You have become high on the height; you rose up as the Benben stone in the Mansion of the Phoenix...."

The import here is clear: Ra-Atum's elevation in the pantheon was equivalent to the Benben's place of honor atop a pyramid.

The **Mansion of the Phoenix** was the name of the great temple at Heliopolis that housed the Benben, the sacred object that came down from the Heavens.

LELA TAO can therefore be said to have "come down" from Infinity to take her seat of honor atop the Day Dream Pyramid in her disunified form as the Witness of our Universe.

CHARACTERISTICS AND RELATIONSHIP

What are the characteristics and relationship of LELA the Dreamer and the Mandala?

❖ LELA the Dreamer can only exist in the Eternal Moment of Now. This permanent state of existence frees her from being burdened with, or influenced by, memories or past information. LELA the Dreamer is a qualitatively different from everyone else: She is the Perfect Witness.

❖ LELA the Dreamer's pure Witnessing Stream of Consciousness -- the literal live feed arising from the totality of our Universe – passes instantaneously in pure form into the Eternal and incorruptible storage Cloud that we call the Cosmic Mandala.

❖ There is no time lag or transcription error in the transmission of content from the Dreamer to the Cloud.

❖ LELA the Dreamer adds nothing to the content she observes and transmits into the Cosmic Mandala. The content is absolutely what it is.

❖ The Cosmic Mandala can only passively record what LELA the Dreamer witnesses. Therefore, no non-existent thing can ever be recorded. Said another way, if a thing can be conceived of in way whatsoever it has some form of existence. This has staggering implications.

❖ The strict limitations of Witnessing and Recording prevent LELA the Dreamer or the Cosmic Mandala from having any experiences of any kind. Their activities are passive.

❖ LELA the Dreamer does not superimpose any model of reality upon the Universe and cannot do so. The Dreamer will see the total Universe without distortion, lies, or ambiguity. She will witness all models of reality without being a part of any model of reality. The Witness has no need to create or devise a model of reality for herself.

❖ The Dreamer Mandala does not superimpose any model of reality upon the Universe nor is it programmed to do so. Conversely, the Cosmic Mandala duly records all models of reality.

Chapter Thirteen

DREAM TRIBE VII:
THE FINAL TRANSFORMATION

We previously symbolized the Dream Tribe as the retinue attending to a sleeping Goddess

We now symbolize the Dream Tribe using the Egyptian image shown above.

This image is used to convey the Dream Tribe disunifying into the continuum of male and female energies that will arise within human Consciousness. We very are careful here to speak only of energies; we have no need to assign male and female energies to chromosomes, gender, or archaic marriage laws.

THE WORK SCENE

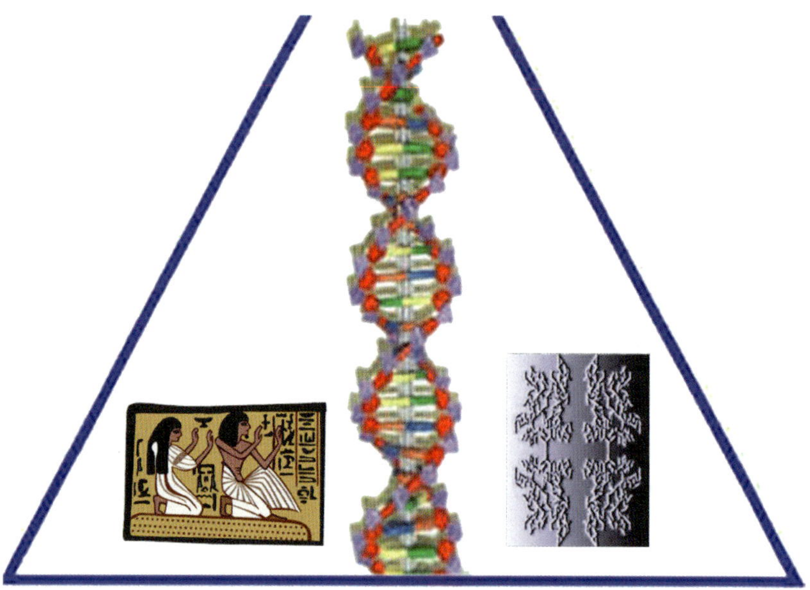

The Work Scene

The objects presented to your view in **_The Work Scene_** comprise the central elements contained in the Day Dream Pyramid:

- ❖ The Jeweled Tower erected from of the Fundamental Forces and the Electromagnetic Spectrum.

- ❖ The Dream Tribe working inside of the Pyramid to transform LELA's Day Dream into our Universe.

- ❖ The Source Codes of Disunification that govern the Disunification. The Source Codes will serve as the basis of self-organization – or what we call the process of Disunification-Evolution in our Universe.

THE FEMALE AND MALE ENERGIES OF INFINITY

Before we ceremonially place the Capstone atop the Day Dream Pyramid, two final additions must be made.

These final additions are my acknowledgement of the wisdom contained in chapter 42 of the *Tao Te Ching*:

The Tao gives birth to One.

One gives birth to Two.

Two gives birth to Three.

Three gives birth to all things.

All things have their backs to the female

and stand facing thc malc.

When male and female combine,

all things achieve harmony.

Ordinary men hate solitude.

But the Master makes use of it,

embracing his aloneness, realizing

he is one with the whole universe.

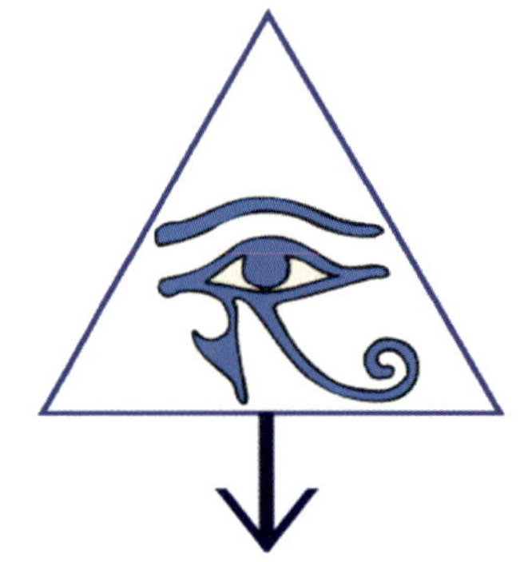

The Masculine energy of Infinity is symbolized by placing a descending arrow beneath the Pyramidion.

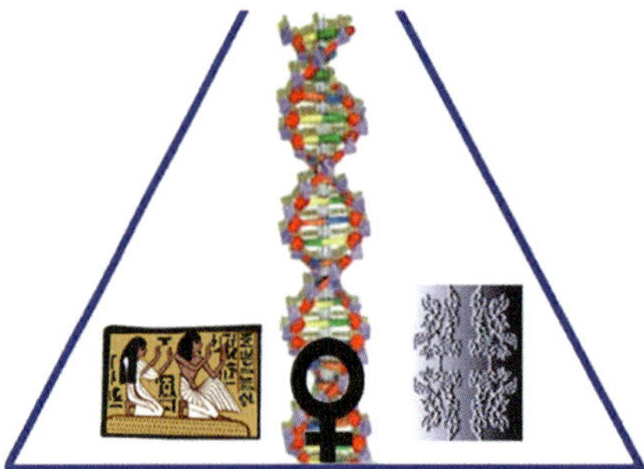

The symbol of the Dream Tribe is placed in the Pyramid.

The Feminine energy of Infinity is then added by using the ♀ symbol.

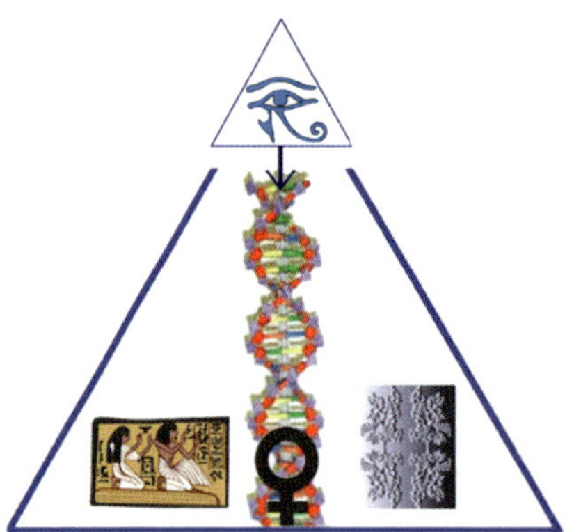

Having been infused with the male and female energies, the Dreamer-Mandala is placed above the main body of the pyramid.

This completes the Day Dream Pyramid.

THE COMPLETED DAY DREAM PYRAMID

The Capstone is set in place.

The Day Dream Pyramid is complete.

A faster-than-light virtual object composed of pure Primal Matter, our ***Minimalist Machine of Consciousness*** is ready to launch.

A note about my computer illustrations: I made these graphics over ten years ago using a fairly simple computer and image processing program. My graphics may be primitive by today's standards, but I keep them because they are original. I also use some of my very old drawings in this book as they show part of what I was trying to capture using my own hand, a blank piece of paper, and a Rapidograph ink pen.

Chapter Fourteen

DREAM TRIBES VIII & IX:

INITIATING THE DISUNIFICATION

The events described in the next three chapters happen instantaneously, in less time than the blink of an eye and certainly much faster than a thief in the night.

The words and symbols are presented in a sequence that allows you to imagine the Disunification of Energy and Awareness.

The Disunification begins when the Dream Tribes enter the Day Dream Pyramid and ascend the Jeweled Tower.

The Disunification will be initiated from the Jeweled Tower.

From their place in the Heart of the Tower, The Dream Tribe performs ***The Ritual of Firelight***, a ceremony solemnizing their departure from Infinity for an Eternity.

The Dream Tribe knows they will not be returning to Infinity until our Universe is over.

In their ritual, the Dream Tribe asks LELA TAO to favor their daring undertaking in which the One becomes the many.

A grand ceremonial fire is lighted and is soon is blazing. The smell of sandalwood incense fills the Pyramid as the Dream Tribe sings in the Fiery Heart of the Pyramid in celebration of Craftwork well done.

We symbolize the firelight in the Heart of the Pyramid by using an image from the Hubble Space Telescope.

The Heart of the Pyramid.

This Hubble photo shows a glowing ring around a black hole in Galaxy NGC 4261.

The glowing ring around the Black Hole ion Galaxy NGC 4261 symbolizes the ***Altar of Fire*** in the Heart of the Pyramid.

The Altar of Fire will be the place where Infinity ends and our Universe begins.

The Altar of Fire in the center of the Jeweled Tower.

The blue circle around the Day Dream Pyramid reminds us that the Pyramid is – and has been since its inception – enclosed inside of a Day Sphere.

The Dream Tribe concentrates the Primal Matter on the Fire Altar in order to collapse it down so that it may be disunified.

The Altar of Fire alludes to the esoteric teaching that if a radical spiritual transformation is to occur, then one's total Life Energies must be concentrated in the Heart using the energy of spiritual fire.

The Dream Tribe will be undergoing the enormous spiritual Ordeal of Disunification into their sub-Infinite forms. The Dream Tribe will emerge on the "other side" in radically different forms. Only the Dreamer will remain intact to witness the total event.

You too will be disunified.

You too will undergo the enormous Ordeal of Disunification.

DISUNIFICATION AS A FASTER-THAN-LIGHT EVENT

The Disunification is a faster-than-light event in which the Primal Matter is crushed down to zero volume and then disunified. Infinity does most of the work; the Source Codes do the rest.

Disunification occurs inside a Day Sphere that is "hermetically" sealed off from Infinity.

In the following sequence of events, the Day Sphere is not symbolized or shown, as it is essentially invisible.

Dream Tribes VIII and IX initiate the process of the Disunification.

Once initiated, the automated Source Codes of Disunification will take over. The process of Disunification is fully automated in its final phases. This automation will continue perpetually in our Universe.

The Dream Tribes begin by flexing and stressing the Pyramid into a Probability Wave.

The Probability Wave is symbolized by twisting the Pyramid in such a way as to emphasize its three corners, or peaks.

These peaks denote the probabilistic quantum-mechanical nature of our Universe.

The flexing and stressing of the Pyramid causes it to lose its structural integrity; the Pyramid swiftly collapses in on itself and transforms into the Bright Star:

The Collapsing Pyramid, from which emerges…

…The Five-Pointed Bright Star.

SORTING THE PRIMAL MATTER

The Source Codes of Disunification engage at this critical juncture in order to sort the Primal Matter contained within the Bright Star.

Sorting is part of the process required to ensure that the Primal Matter will be released in an ***exact sequence*** during the Disunification.

The sorting operation causes the Bright and Morning Star to undergo a transition in which it becomes the **Scanned Star.**

The Scanned Star is rendered as existing inside of scan lines.

The concept here is that the Source Codes are "scanning, sorting, and aligning" the Primal Matter in preparation for Disunification.

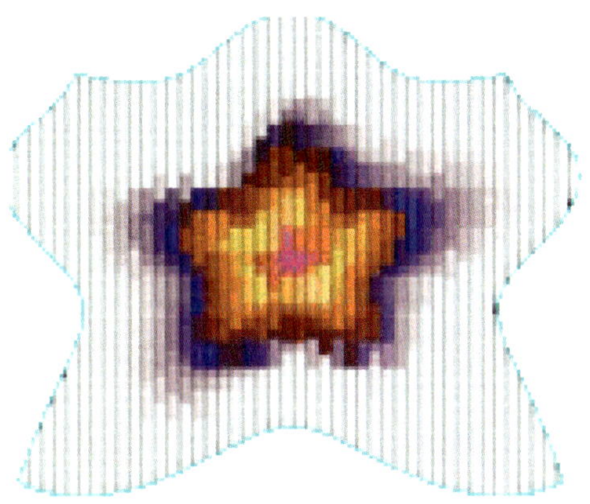

THE PRE-RADIOACTIVE STAR

The Scanned Star now approaches the Relativity Horizon.

Once the Star crosses this horizon, it will be disunified and disappear from Infinity.

Relativity is not an allowed condition in the Unity of Infinity. Relativity is permitted only within the interior of sub-Infinite universes.

On the edge of the Relativity Horizon, the Digitized Star suddenly enters an intense pre-radioactive state:

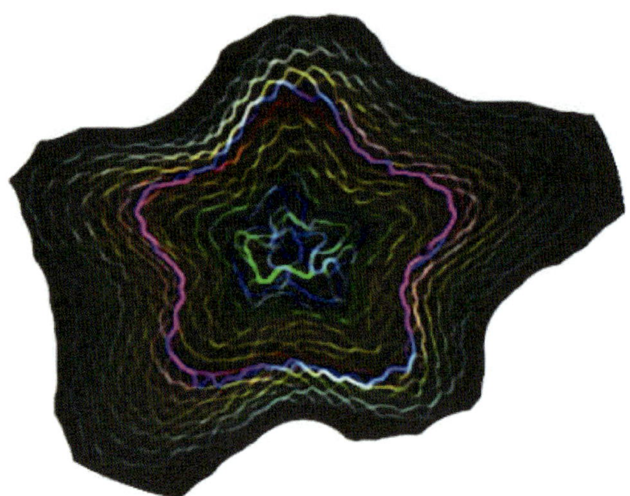

The Pre-Radioactive Star

THE SWIRLING VORTEX

Due to the dangerously unstable state of the Pre-Radioactive Star, Infinity hyper-compresses it into a swirling vortex.

This hyper-compression drastically increases the heat and density of the Star and flattens it into a swirling vortex whose mass is located at the center:

The Swirling Vortex

The flattening of the Star causes it to internally fracture. This highly structured fracturing breaks critical symmetries, thus allowing the 10+ "unpackaging dimensions" needed for Disunification to deploy from within the Primal Matter.

Driven by hyper-compression, the unpackaging of its 10+ internal dimensions, and it's incredibly high energy density, the Pre-Radioactive Star begins a cyclonic rotation at faster-than-light velocity as its internal physics seek equilibrium in a radical non-equilibrium state.

The Dream Tribe inside the Star senses their approaching annihilation into oblivion.

The Dream Tribe is now lost and can no longer navigate or exactly remember the Dream, for they too are collapsing under the Onslaught of Disunification, their memories and futures falling apart before their gaze. Only the Witness remains intact and can see all that is arising.

The Source Codes take over. The Star is now on autopilot with the black box recording everything.

BLUE EYE

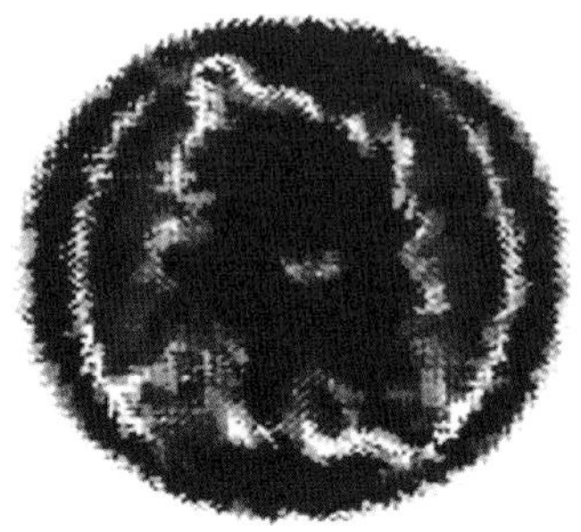

The Sphere with the Dreamer at the Center

The swirling vortex buckles and disintegrates into a sphere of near-zero volume.

A single point, ***Blue Eye***, rests upon the broken Altar.

Blue Eye symbolizes LELA the Dreamer who alone witnesses this great unfolding drama of Disunification.

THE BLACK PEARL

The Blue Eye suddenly implodes into the superheated, super-dense ***Black Pearl***.

The Black Pearl is the ***Singularity-Seed*** of our Universe.

The Primal Matter massed within the Black Pearl is so enormously concentrated that it has to do something; it cannot remain in this state.

There are now only two possible allowed states for the Black Pearl.

It must either collapse back into the Unity of Infinity, or, it must disunify and become a sub-Infinite bubble Universe.

SECTION III

OPENING PANDORA'S BOX

THE DAY DREAM PYRAMID

The day after my car ride up into the San Gabriel Mountains, I wrote a text I now call **The Original Description**. This text became the seed out of which Disunification Cosmology grew.

THE ORIGINAL DESCRIPTION

The Dreamer wrestles with the flux of infinite imagination. In the stillness of the primordial night, in the dream, there is desire. Labyrinthine patterns of blue and gold, of emerald and silver, form a dazzling polychrome train that swirls downward into the void of the dreaming pool. Sizzling electricity dances on mirrors in the darkness. A riot of sound, the babble of billions of tongues, the cacophony of instruments, animals, fire, wind and water resonates with the arabesque of image.

The flames begin to burn into the very fabric of Infinity. As Infinity burns, it illumines the Void with tremendous light. The dream begins to appear.

There is desire. Blue-gray islands of clouds rise from the floor of newly cut fiords and reach beckoningly into the cold black heaven of the solar lights in a last attempt to preserve Unity. But it is fruitless, for desire rises. The tall forests and strong mountains call out to the marshes on the horizon. Blazing wind-whipped canyons snake to the lowlands and dump their rivers into the seas. The dream of creation can no longer be resisted.

Liquid eyes and sinew on bone, fur and claws in wet rock and wood: Velvety animals prowl the desire-lands. Bright red and gold become slippery fish and fantastic birds; deep blue and silver streaks the faces of reptiles. The allure of worlds, the power and sensuality, the embrace of this dream of consequences arouses the passion of that One dreaming. Brighter and brighter the fire grows as desire intensifies and the infinite sky begins to collapse and fall into the Void.

There is desire. Supple flesh, soft hair, white teeth, pounding heart, and bright eyes: There is suddenly another, a lover, and the lover says, "Come to me." The lovers embrace: Sensuous firm breasts, beautiful hips, moist lips, bright searching eyes; a broad chest, strong arms, gentle hands, eyes searching eyes. There is desire for union, for passion. The lovers caress and there is union. Their rhythm builds towards an inevitable climax of blinding fire. Infinity swells and grows blue-hot in the dream darkness. Light is thrown across the face of the deep. A white arc jumps across a black gap.

There is desire, and then the explosion of light within itself into the scream of awakening chaos! The void cleaves Infinity in two and scatters the Energy and Awareness that had given it birth. Virgin light is thrown into the night, into the abyss of the vacuum and the paradox of time.

Energy and Awareness, the very essence of the Dreamer, pours unreservedly from that One into the unfolding of the spacetime dreamscape. Fleeing as if had seen another, disunified Awareness races out in every direction towards the spherical vanishing point and ultimate disappearance.

At some point in their expansion into nothingness, disunified Energy and Awareness recoils against the elastic tension of a mysterious spherical wall. Tremendous waves of force are generated as disunified Energy and Awareness decelerate against the pressure of their own expansion and turn back into the center. The rampant disunified Energy and Awareness churns and froths as it it were a magical elixir in the cauldron of a sorceress. Whirlpools appear in the unstable pressure zones and compress Energy and Awareness into superheated funnels. Tensioned Energy and Awareness, caught in the circular, hyper-velocities of the funnels, yield the first pristine colors and voices of the stellar dawn.

The funnels serve as centrifuges to separate out Energy from Awareness. The two primal forces of Infinity, once intertwined as the eternal stream of LELA, are channeled off into the secret conduits of the universe. Encoded within each of the streams are the patterns of intelligence and the desire needed to animate the dream: The complexities of form, process, and being; the ability to repeat form; and the drive to survive and create have been burned into the night.

Disunified Energy is quickly knotted into the helical spectra of galaxies while Awareness awakens into profound ignorance with a scream that shakes the Void: The Dream has become real and now there is no turning back, for the Dreamer has passed into oblivion. This scream will both haunt and inspire the Void forevermore as it echoes throughout the ages and resonates in the heart of every sentient being.

As the first star clusters and beings arise, the angels of the morning sing and the stars rise in radiant glory. Seraphim shine brightly in the firmament of heaven and ask, "Who is the great power behind this marvel? Who is the One who sets beyond the stars?"

A solitary figure stands on a beach in a distant land and beholds the body: Hands, breath, and sight, this one stands upright listening to a faint, almost imperceptible echo that can be heard above the crashing surf. This one is troubled by the echo and doesn't know why. Then, as the figure gazes into the endless sky, a terrifying, undeniable realization strikes: "Oh my God, I exist!"

Chapter Fifteen

THE DISUNIFICATION OF
ENERGY & AWARENESS

The Black Pearl is now at the Relativity Horizon.

Inevitability is demanded: The Black Pearl must collapse back down to Infinity or disunify and become one of the countless universes into the Multiverse.

Once the "strings are cut" the Black Pearl will become unbound from Infinity and the Disunification will begin. Pandora's Box will open and the Primal Matter will race out into the Void with guns blazing against the unfolding and all-encompassing gravity.

The sound of a wooden gavel banging down on a marble sounding block is suddenly heard.

The sound of the gavel resonates across the Empyrean and serves notice that Disunification is to proceed.

The Dream Tribe Lodge is now open for the purpose of conducting the Third Degree of Universe-Making. In this degree, the Lodge will be operating at faster-than-light speed.

Of this, take due notice and govern yourself accordingly.

Only LELA the Dreamer will witness the actual Disunification.

THE FINAL INRUSH

As the gavel bangs down on the sounding block to open the Dream Tribe Lodge, the Black Pearl now stands alone in the Day Sphere.

This place is the Doorway between Infinity and the Multiverse.

Seeing the Black Pearl fully ready to be a new universe, Infinity floods the Day Sphere with an incalculable amount of Surplus Energy to initiate *Sequence Alpha: The Disunification*.

This flood of **Surplus Energy** is called the **Final Inrush** and is symbolized as three golden waves in a black field:

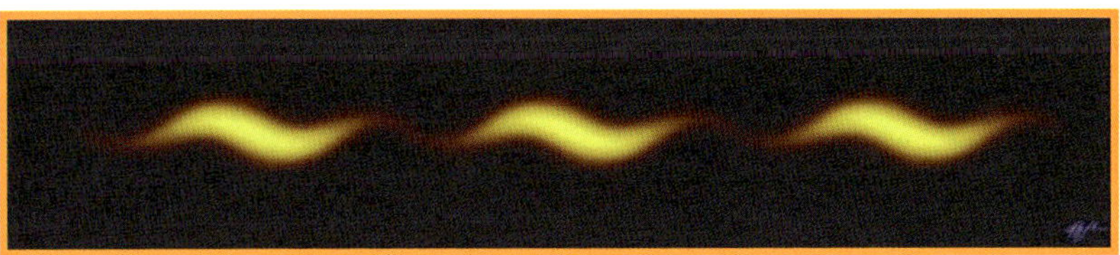

The Final Inrush causes the Black Pearl to become a molten sphere that shines brighter than a trillion-trillion massed stars.

The energy from the Final Inrush races into the molten Black Pearl and breaks the remaining symmetries deep in its interior.

The molten Black Pearl suddenly and catastrophically explodes in the ***Day Rise Trinity Explosion.***

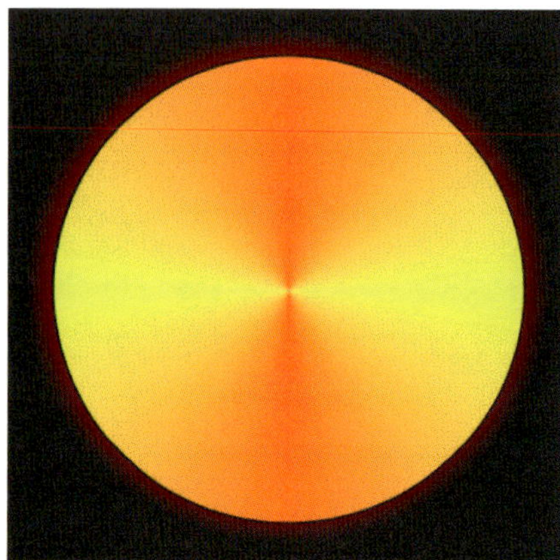

The Molten Black Pearl

On our side of things, the Day Rise Trinity Explosion would indeed be seen as the Big Bang that initiated and expanded our Universe from an infinitesimally small and inexplicable singularity.

The Day Sphere is elastic and – driven by the pressure of the Day Rise Trinity Explosion – instantaneously hyper-expands out in all directions.

ˋDISUNIFICATION REACTORS

We characterize Day Spheres as "Disunification Reactors" inside of which relativistic, sub-Infinite Universes can occur.

Thus, the Final Inrush was the opposite of scramming, or flooding a nuclear reactor core with water to shut it down if it approaches meltdown.

In this case, Infinity flooded the Black Pearl with a colossal amount of Surplus Energy sufficient to trigger the Disunification.

Unlike a nuclear reactor that would meltdown if additional power were put into when it became dangerously unstable in a criticality event, our **Day-Sphere-Universe** was able to instantaneously hyper-expand in response to the enormous surplus energy of the Disunification Event.

Relativity, motion, and other sub-Infinite physics thereafter arose inside of our bubble universe per the Source Codes of Disunification.

The sum total of the Primal Matter and energy in our Universe was transferred from Infinity.

This high capacity, high-energy, highly-stable transfer converted some small part of Infinity into our universe. This is Disunification in essence.

THE RELEASE OF THE PRIMAL MATTER

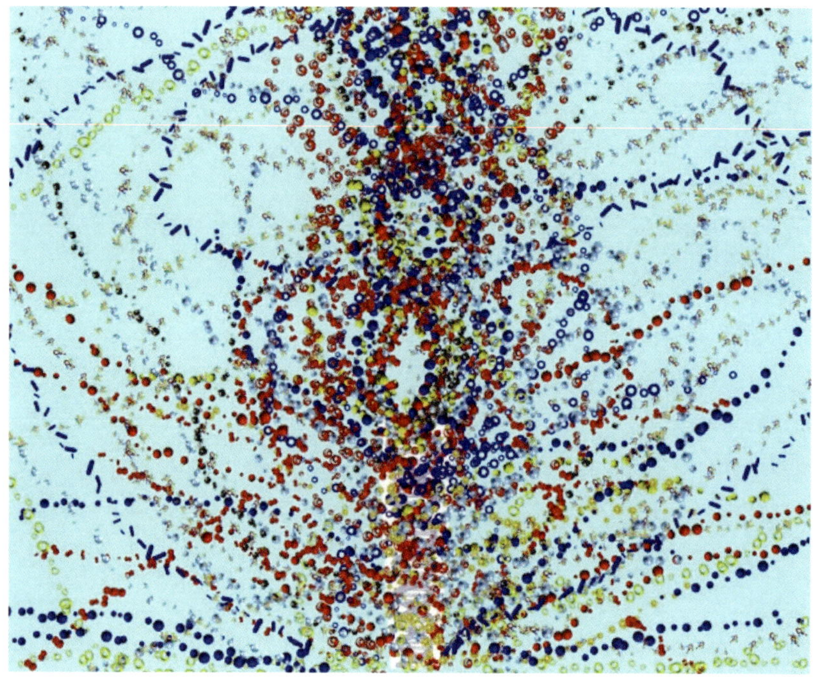

The Sandstorm

We symbolize the release of the Primal Matter with the symbol shown above.

The name of the symbol is ***The Sandstorm.***

NOTES ON THE DISUNIFICATION

1. The Disunification unpackaged the Primal Matter that was contained within a superluminal-transdimensional transport vehicle known as the Black Pearl.

2. The10+ "unpackaging dimensions" were deployed first.

3. Time and Space were deployed ahead of the Primal Matter. This allowed the rest of the Primal Matter to be unpackaged.

4. The "Final Inrush" of energy into our Universe shows that Infinity used more energy to disunify our Universe than our Universe contains. Like any other sub-Infinite system, then, the Disunification Event had system losses.

5. After our Universe dropped to C, the speed of light constant, the energy from the Disunification continued to expand space. This expansion continues today and is in fact accelerating as a function of the "unpackaging pressures" exerted by the force of Disunification-Evolution.

6. Because Energy cannot be created or destroyed, Disunification Cosmology states that the Energy in our Universe could have only come from the external source of Infinity. Our Universe is constrained by physical laws. Thus, it could not have created its own Energy and violated physical laws. An external event was required. This event was the Disunification of Energy and Awareness.

7. Disunification Cosmology is a cosmological and metaphysical alternative that redefines the Big Bang as the high-energy event called the Disunification of Energy and Awareness.

8. The Disunification hyper-expanded the Day Sphere so that early Space increased at faster-than-light speed in order to contain the disunifying (and equally faster-than-light) Primal Matter

Chapter Sixteen

The Mystery Ship

J. Augustine

DISUNIFYING STRINGS & SOULS

The Disunification event was *Superluminal Automata.*

The Black Pearl was a faster-than-light-virtual-machine decelerating from Infinite speed in order to morph into a bubble universe.

Just as a sonic boom is created when the speed of sound is broken by a jet aircraft, Day Teaching posits that a "Big Bang" occurs when a faster-than-light-virtual-machine decelerates to the speed of light.

Having decelerated, the Black Pearl first deployed spacetime into which it then disunified and unpackaged the Primal Matter. The region of slowing to light speed comprises the ***Transitional Chaos State***.

This state is also a faster-than-light phase of the Disunification during which our Universe was transitioning from its virtual existence in Infinity to its actual sub-finite existence within the Multiverse.

This state was one of great chaos and symmetry breaking as the Black Pearl converted into the early Universe of Higgs bosons and quark-gluon plasma, and the **Protogenoi**, primeval forms of Consciousness explored in chapter twenty-two.

There was a Big Bang as the Black Pearl entered the Void.

Day Teaching re-conceptualizes the "Big Bang" as the instantaneous unpackaging of the total contents of the Black Pearl. This unpackaging process generated tremendous heat that contributed to the hyper-expansion of our early Universe.

To say that the Primal Matter was "unpackaged" or "disunified" means that it was unpackaged and disunified in an exact manner. We directly borrow from string physics and thus posit that there were 10+ or more dimensions present at the beginning of the Big Bang.

We say that faster-than-light speed and extra unpackaging dimensions would be needed to accomplish the Disunification. Moreover, time and space would also be disunified from Infinity as part of the two Disunification events discussed in this chapter:

- ❖ **Faster-than-Light Multidimensional Unpackaging of the Primal Matter**

- ❖ **The Unpackaging of Time and Space Coincident with the Primal Matter**

FASTER–THAN–LIGHT
MULTIDIMENSIONAL UNPACKAGING

String theory informs us that 10+ dimensions are present in our Universe, but that we can only "see" three: Length, width, and depth.

Einstein added time as a dimension to get Spacetime.

String theory states that the other dimensions are so small or "rolled up" that we cannot detect them. Persuaded by string theory, Disunification Cosmology maintains that there were numerous dimensions active during the Disunification event.

These dimensions included time and space, for time and space had to be disunified, or unpackaged, first in order for the Primal Matter to have space and time into which it could unpackage.

We consider that the region of "pre-Planck time" was a superluminal pre-quantum-mechanical state wherein the virtual Black Pearl was transiting from Infinity into the energized vacuum of unpackaging space in our Universe.

Even as the Day Rise Trinity Explosion blew apart the Black Pearl and pushed the Primal Matter into the expanding Day Sphere, the tremendous force of "Unpackaging Gravity" also acted to pull the Primal Matter from Infinity.

Thus, the Primal Matter was both pushed and pulled from Infinity.

When the Disunification occurred, a multidimensional portal between Infinity and our Universe existed at above light speed for a brief fraction of time.

This portal was "made of" the unpackaging dimensions that served as the Multidimensional Superhighway along which the Primal Matter blazed along as it disunified from the Black Pearl.

We consider that some of these "unpackaging dimensions" were only viable at faster-than-light speeds as our Universe was disunifying from Infinity.

As such, these extra collapsed when our Universe slowed to the speed of light.

Predictively, our Universe will end in a faster-than-light Reunification in which these dimensions will reappear once again above the speed of light in order to upload our completed Universe back into Infinity.

While Day Teaching is metaphysical in nature, string theory makes a great deal of intuitive sense. For this reason, we posit that some of the unpackaging dimensions were "folded up" and stored in undetectable dimensions following the Disunification, this as part of the good housekeeping of our physical Universe.

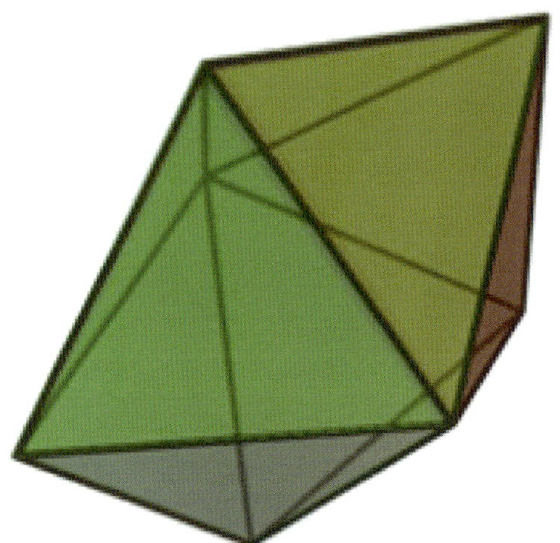

A pentagonal dipyramid (one of the Johnson solids) portrays the unfolding of the many dimensions in the first instant of our Universe.

With its ten triangular faces, fifteen sides, and seven vertices, this solid suggests the >10 dimensions that were operative in the Transitional Chaos State.

THE UNPACKAGING OF TIME AND SPACE:

THE UNIVERSE SLOWS TO THE SPEED OF LIGHT

Following the faster-than-light Disunification, our Universe dropped to an energy state that allowed C, the speed of light constant, to become operative.

Time and Space unpackaged and interlocked to form the extremely stable state of the Universe that we call ***C Compliant Spacetime***.

A special set of physics would be needed to describe the Disunification of Energy and Awareness. I am definitely not the one to write the Physics of Disunification if indeed they can ever be written.

In terms of Consciousness, once the Life Awareness left Infinity it became **disunified Awareness**. This resulted in every possible thought, imagination, fantasy nightmare, and desire being liberated from Infinity. That is why I wrote in my ***Original Description***:

> "The Dreamer wrestles with the flux of infinite imagination. In the stillness of the primordial night, in the dream, there is desire. Labyrinthine patterns of blue and gold, of emerald and silver, form a dazzling polychrome train that swirls downward into the void of the dreaming pool. Sizzling electricity dances on mirrors in the darkness. A riot of sound, the babble of billions of tongues, the cacophony of instruments, animals, fire, wind and water resonates with the arabesque of image."

Human Consciousness reflects the Infinite Consciousness disunified, evolved, and still evolving into its endless forms across time.

The next chapter introduces the key concept of **Disunification-Evolution**.

In the Disunification,

the Day Dream Pyramid

was instantly vaporized

into the Cloud of Life

by the Great Light

and Thunderclap.

Come with me then

and Witness the Zep Tepi.

Chapter Seventeen

The Disunification Mandala

J. Augustine

DISUNIFICATION-EVOLUTION

Day Teaching reconceptualizes and expands the concept of Evolution by introducing the concept of **Disunification-Evolution**.

The abbreviated form of Disunification-Evolution is spelled "**Day-Ev**" and the word is pronounced ***Day-Yev***.

All of the Primal Matter in the Universe disunified from a central, finite point called the Black Pearl located inside the Day Sphere.

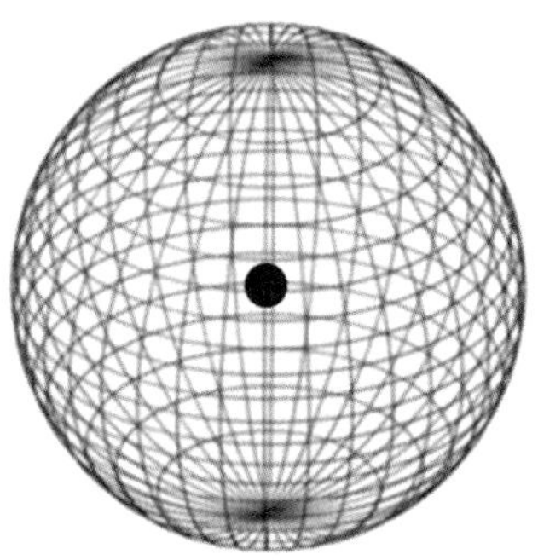

Following the Disunification, the Primal Matter of Consciousness and Energy began to energetically expand outward in every direction from the central point.

The sum total of forces exerted by the engine of Disunification-Evolution acting upon the Universe is called **unpackaging pressure**.

Disunification-Evolution is the universal engine that works across all scales to unpackage, unfold, and evolve the Primal Matter from simplicity into complexity per the Source Codes.

Disunification-Evolution and its relentless unpackaging pressure is symbolized by **Four Corners**, a Day Sphere with four lines emanating out from the center.

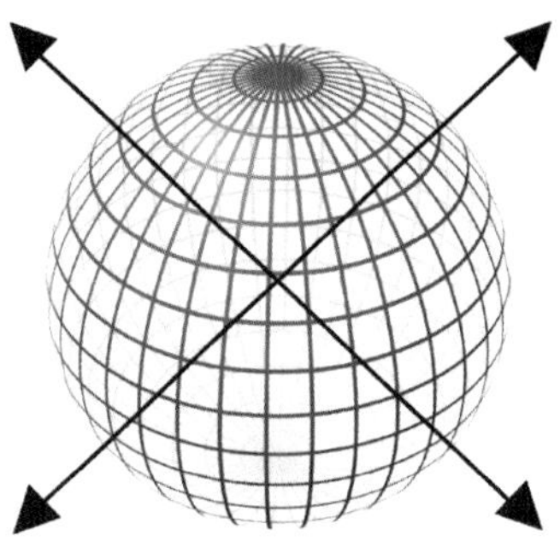

In Day Teaching, we use Four Corner diagrams to illustrate the dynamic – and often agonizing – range of forces that arise in Consciousness and Energy.

The relentless unpackaging pressure of Day-Ev works inexorably and ruthlessly to unpackage and evolve all forms, processes, and beings.

We all feel and directly experience the unpackaging pressure in various ways as stress, anxiety, terror, agitation, problem-solving, impatience, relentlessness, completion, and sometimes we experience it as Love and the pure Joy of Creation.

One of the ultimate human goals must be to control the engine of Disunification-Evolution rather than having it control us. This will and must happen.

THE FUNDAMENTAL FORCES ARE UNPACKAGED

The singular massive example of Disunification-Evolution exerting massive unpackaging pressure is shown in the unfolding of the fundamental forces following the Disunification.

In the CERN diagram we see how the early Universe unpackaged itself:

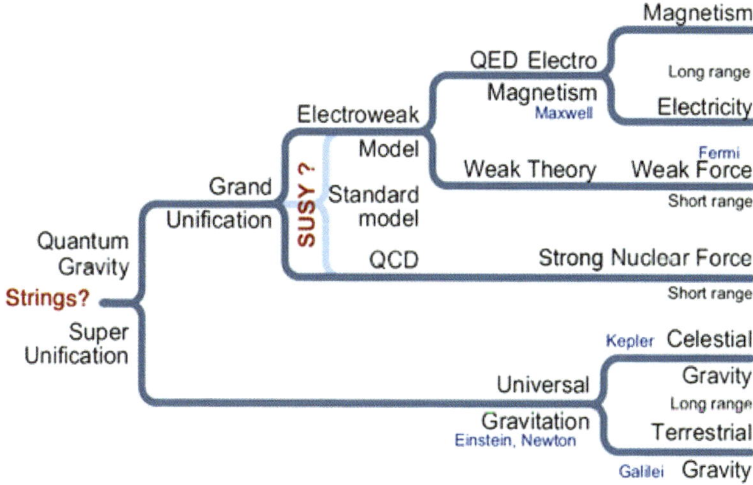

We use the CERN[10] diagram to illustrate the Disunification and unpackaging of the fundamentals forces in the first instant of our Universe.

The diagram is read from left to right. It depicts our early Universe in what Science calls a state of **Super Unification**.

---

[10] Image retrieved in 2010 at
http://cms.web.cern.ch/cms/Physics/Supersymmetry/index.html

We take the CERN diagram to represent the first instant of Disunification-Evolution.

Hence, Super-Unification would be the state of the Universe just as it exited the Unity of Infinity and before massive symmetry-breaking occurred.

Because Disunification-Evolution energetically unpackages Primal Matter, Disunification-Evolution must of necessity be symmetry-breaking at times. This occurs in both Consciousness and Mater

There was symmetry breaking as all of the fundamental forces were being unpackaged and deployed in the logical and sequential matter dictated by the Source Codes.

Stated another way, our Universe is anthropically constrained, as will be described.

In terms of a Unified Theory, Day Teaching argues that Infinity alone is unified on a grand scale.

Therefore, any Theory of Everything must comprehend Infinity.

Moreover, it follows that everything in our Universe is fundamentally made out of only one thing and that one thing is Infinity.

The Disunification resulted in the one thing being disunified into countless sub-Infinite forms, processes, and beings that are all functionally differentiated from one another.

Infinity and the Multiverse therefore comprise a **Unity-Nonunity** state.

THE ANTHROPIC PRINCIPLE

Disunification-Evolution is conceptually akin to the notion of the "anthropic principle," a term coined in 1974 by noted British cosmologist Brandon Carter.

The anthropic principle argues that our Universe was – choose your word – designed, fine-tuned, or constrained, in such a way as to allow for human life.

Princeton University website offers this description of the Anthropic Principle:

> "In physics and cosmology, the anthropic principle is the philosophical argument that observations of the physical Universe must be compatible with the conscious life that observes it. Some proponents of the argument reason that it explains why the Universe has the age and the fundamental physical constants necessary to accommodate conscious life. As a result, they believe that the fact that the Universe's fundamental constants are within the narrow range thought to allow life is not remarkable.

> "The principle was formulated as a response to a series of observations that the laws of nature and parameters of the Universe take on values that are consistent with conditions for life as we know it rather than a set of values that would not be consistent with life as observed on Earth. The anthropic principle states that this phenomenon is a necessity because living observers wouldn't be able to exist, and hence, observe the Universe, were these laws and constants not constituted in this way.[11]"

Disunification Teaching maintains that our Universe is fine-tuned by Infinity, and so this is why our Universe is exactly the way it is.

---

[11] Retrieved online at:
http://www.princeton.edu/~achaney/tmve/wiki100k/docs/Anthropic_principle.html

Our Universe was not predetermined, but the Primal Matter was "anthropically constrained" so that it could be disunified and evolved within the parameters defined in the Source Codes.

In other words, when the structure is there, the details take care of themselves.

For example, while the process of Disunification systematically evolved and configured the highly evolved human body over time in response to environmental conditions and demands, what happens in any given life is another matter altogether.

Moreover, while humans evolved to be inventors, what we invent is not predetermined. However, what we invent must follow the path of the physical world, i.e. we cannot invent anything that violates natural laws. However, we can and do modify the raw materials in our physical world into inventions that can be very binding and deadly. There are no "natural laws" against inventing any harmful thing.

In this sense, Humanity follows the path of Consciousness, i.e. we cannot be anything other than Consciousness itself. However, we can and do modify Consciousness into very binding and punitive forms such as Identity and Ideology. Again, there are no "natural laws" against inventing any harmful thing.

THE BBISBE MODEL

Current materialistic thinking posits a complex, all-encompassing, naturalistic scenario that I call the *"Big Bang-into-Stellar-and-Biological-Evolution"* model.

The acronym ***Bbisbe*** (pronounced Biz-Bee) is used to abbreviate the name of this cosmological model.

The Bbisbe model describes an atheistic, unaccountably caused, spontaneous Big Bang event that self-organized itself into our highly structured biological world. The evolutionary mechanics from stars to biological life is conceptually understood. We see it in terms of the anthropic nature of Disunification.

In their co-authored book, ***The Grand Design***, Stephen Hawking and Leonard Mlodinow state in the introduction that our Universe is "just one of many universes that appeared spontaneously out of nothing, each with different laws of nature."[12]

As materialists, Hawking and Mlodinow invoke a ***spontaneous appearance out of nothing*** as their ultimate notion of how our Universe and all other universes began.

Hawking declared philosophy to be dead at the Google Zeitgeist Conference in 2011, and yet we see his notion of spontaneous creation as characteristic of the inherent quasi-philosophy demanded by physics itself.

In my mind, Newtonian mechanics is to Physics what quantum-mechanics is to quasi-philosophy. When Hawking and Mlodinow discuss the Multiverse in ***The Grand Design***, they must also invoke spontaneous creation as their quasi-philosophical statement of Ultimacy.

Conversely, we do not accept a strict Bbisbe model of spontaneous creation.

---

[12] Stephen Hawking and Leonard Mlodinow, The Grand Design, Bantam Books, 2011.

Instead, we explain the apparent spontaneous appearance of our Universe and of all universes by asserting three points:

❖ Infinity sourced our Universe and all other universes

❖ Human religious claims have nothing whatsoever to do with the appearance of our Universe

❖ Disunification-Evolution is the engine that drives the expansion and self-assembly of our Universe into all forms, processes, and beings.

Chapter Eighteen

THE CONVERSIONS OF ENERGY & CONSCIOUSNESS

Primal Matter Evolving into Forms

J. Augustine

Disunification-Evolution is about unfolding, unpackaging, and fully exploring the Primal Matter.

Each new universe in the Multiverse allows LELA TAO to take some different fraction of Infinity apart so that she can experience herself not as the Divine One, but rather from the point of view of sub-Infinite forms, processes, and beings.

What LELA needs to make universes is Energy.

What LELA needs to experience universes is Consciousness.

THE SPECTRUM OF CONSCIOUSNESS

When Infinity disunified, part of it disunified into the *Spectrum of Consciousness*.

The electromagnetic spectrum serves as an analogy to illustrate what is meant by "the Spectrum of Consciousness."

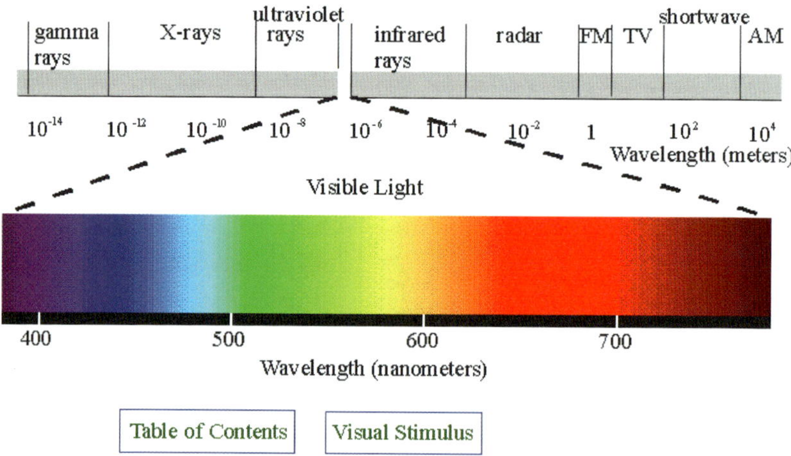

Just as the electromagnetic spectrum was harvested from Infinity and disunified into our Universe, so too was the Spectrum of Consciousness. The electromagnetic spectrum contains all possible "colors" in the Universe – including those colors within visible light (VIS) that we can see.

In like manner, the Spectrum of Consciousness contains the totality of all of the "colors" that exist within Consciousness.

Disunified Awareness unfolded into all of the different "Colors of Consciousness" in the Spectrum. Thus, we have love and hate, good and evil, and all of the dualities, polarities, and opposites that exist within the Spectrum of Consciousness.

CONVERSION MECHANICS

Conversion mechanics is the basis of our disunified Universe.

Einstein used his famous equation $E=MC^2$ to describe his discovery that Energy and Mass are convertible. "Convertible" means that matter and energy can be converted into each other:

$$\text{Energy} \leftrightarrow \text{Matter}$$

Day Teaching posits by analogy that ***Consciousness*** and ***Identity*** are convertible:

$$\text{Consciousness} \leftrightarrow \text{Identity}$$

This means that Consciousness and Identity are two distinctly different things:

❖ Consciousness has no central identity but rather exists as the Transpersonal Spectrum of Consciousness from which all identities arise.

❖ Identity is Consciousness contracted, bound, and converted into the individual identity of a particular individual. Any identity represents only a small fraction of the Spectrum of Consciousness. Identity is a discrete "wavelength."

The Spectrum of Consciousness therefore expresses a ***Personal-Transpersonal Duality***:

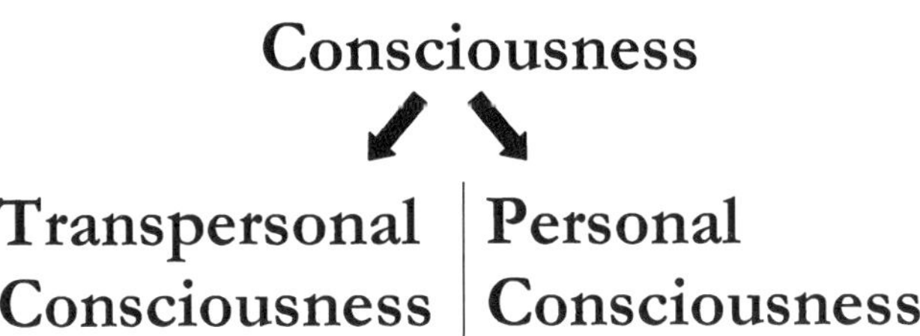

The term "Transpersonal" is used in approximately the same way as used by Transpersonal Psychology, i.e. to speak of the higher regions and potentials within human Consciousness.

Human Consciousness has a Personal-Transpersonal range, or expanse. When this range is not recognized as such, it is misunderstood and thus experienced as a duality or a dilemma.

For example, a personal identity is problematic insofar as it is a limitation and a barrier to knowing the fullness of disunified Consciousness and the resulting freedom that comes from this knowledge.

A personal identity cannot be enlightened – it can only be defended; it can only make itself right by making others wrong. A personal identity is a zero sum game in which one must win and others must lose. A personal identity is a series of continual frustrations and conflicts arising within Consciousness. Lose your identity and the frustrations and conflicts diminish.

To "lose one's self" is to journey into the realm of the Transpersonal Consciousness. Transpersonal Consciousness is the "Ocean of Consciousness" or what has traditionally been called Non-Self. Transpersonal Consciousness has no central identity: It just is.

Personal Consciousness is identity. Personal Consciousness is defined as the karmic "I" we experience as the ego.

One is fundamentally a person; this is existentially inescapable. However, we explicitly decouple personhood from all forms of identity. Personhood is fundamentally Consciousness and identity is a product of conversion mechanics. To the degree that one does not understand the conversion of Consciousness into Identity, they will be trapped by their identity, and this where identity = ego.

The sense of "I" that we each experience is generated from the interaction of the Personal and the Transpersonal. However, most people tend to only experience their personal side.

You have the entire vast range of Consciousness within you.

To the extent that you recoil from your own vastness, however, you contract down to an identity and thus live and behave in a way that is contrary to Disunification-Evolution.

One of Day Teaching's goals is to therefore give you an understanding of your own expanse.

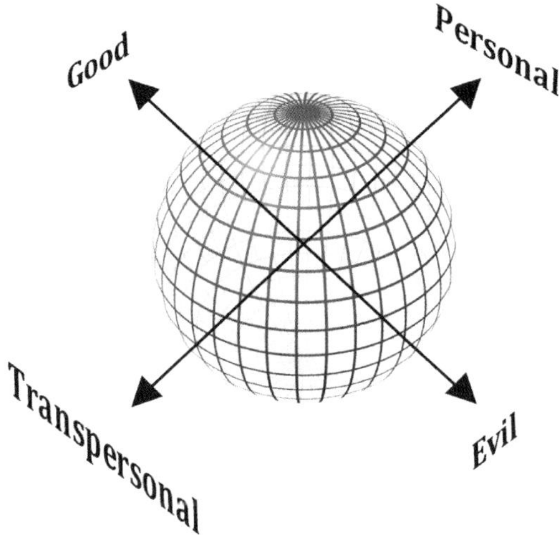

The diagram shown above depicts just one part of the vast expanse of Consciousness as it unfolded in the Disunification.

Humanity has not been able to comprehend its own vastness and so it has created an extensive mythological and religious tradition that posits a Universe at war between Good and Evil.

There is no eternal war between Good and Evil; there is only Disunification-Evolution forcing choices and enforcing consequences.

THE TABLE OF DISUNIFIED AWARENESS

The Spectrum of Consciousness contains far more than just Good and Evil. To give you a wider sense of the Spectrum, we conceptually borrow from the majestic Periodic Table of the Elements. Our table is called the ***Table of disunified Awareness***.

1 Transpersonal Awareness	**Table of Disunified Awareness** Jeffrey Augustine 2013		**2** Self-Awareness
3 Fear of the Other			**4** Embodiment
5 Emotional Reactivity	**6** Good	**7** Evil	**8** Invention
9 Identities	**10** Sins and Taboos	**11** Hate	**12** Logic
13 Hierarchies	**14** Family	**15** Greed	**16** Intuition
17 Religion-Making	**18** Tribalism	**19** Envy	**20** Empiricsim
21 Ideology-Making	**22** Nationalism	**23** Violence	**24** Science
26 War-Making	**27** Globalism	**28** Hyper-Predation	**29** Hyper-Surveillance

Our "periodic table" of disunified Awareness, or **"dATable"** for short, illustrates the ways in which disunified Awareness became discretely expressed in human behavior and that of all other sentient beings arising within the Spectrum of Consciousness.

The dATable of disunified Awareness is not literal in the same way that the periodic table is literal. While we show twenty-nine "Elements of Consciousness" we could just as easily list thousands. The descriptions and number of elements are not as important as the central emphases of the dATable:

❖ Disunified Awareness, or Consciousness, "converted" into all of the identity-based beings in our Universe. For example, Divinities, gods, angels, demons, humans, and elementals are identity-based beings.

❖ Because identities are created from Consciousness, all identities can be converted back into Consciousness. Knowing this fact alone will allow you to reinvent yourself. You have no obligation to be stuck with an identity you do not like being once you know how to convert back into Consciousness.

❖ Disunified Awareness accounts for the "Chemistry of Personality" inherent in all of the beings in our Universe.

❖ Each of the elements on the dATable Periodic Table of disunified Awareness corresponds to a different vibrational energy, or "color" arising within Consciousness.

❖ Each of the "colors" in the Periodic Table of disunified Awareness can be biased, or skewed, towards Good or Evil. It all depends upon the individual.

❖ You never need fear a ghost or any other spirit when you realize they are simply identities. You can refer such identities back into their prior State of Consciousness.

The dATable speaks to archetypes, Heaven and Hell, and the other discrete spiritual states, religions, abstractions, ideologies, and all other mental and spiritual objects contained within Personal-Transpersonal Consciousness.

IDENTITIES & DISUNIFICATION

The Table of disunified Awareness speaks to the Divinities, angels, demons, human, extraterrestrials and all other identities in our Universe.

Divinities are sub-Infinite identities; they are personal forms of Consciousness. Conversely, archetypes are transpersonal patterns arising within Consciousness. Divinities are neither infinite nor omniscient.

Divinities are covered in chapter twenty-two; Creation stories, or what we call Disunification Narratives, in chapter twenty-three.

No matter – it all arises in Consciousness and that is what we want to notice. Never believe that any identity in Heaven or Earth is ultimately real, because it is not. Only Consciousness is real.

All identities are ultimately Psycho-Synthetic and so they come together and fall apart over time. Identities ultimately exist to unpackage Primal Matter. As such, identities are limited and should be transcended over time. When you are done being your present identity, you become enlightened and are free to move on and reinvent yourself.

TURNING CRAYON BOXES UPSIDE DOWN

If we consider the Periodic Table of the Elements and the dATable to be big boxes of crayons, we would do what all children do: We would turn these big boxes upside down in order to free all of the crayons. When we turn the Periodic Table upside down, hydrogen and helium come out first and the heavy metals come out last:

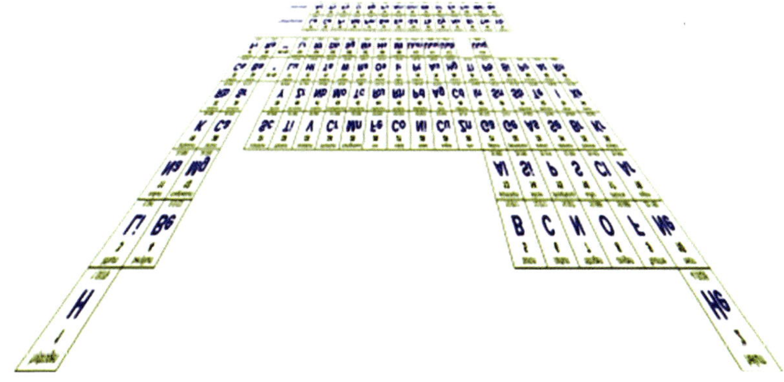

When we turn the dATable upside down, box, the most primitive states of Consciousness come out first. The heavier and more complex forms of Consciousness fall out over time.

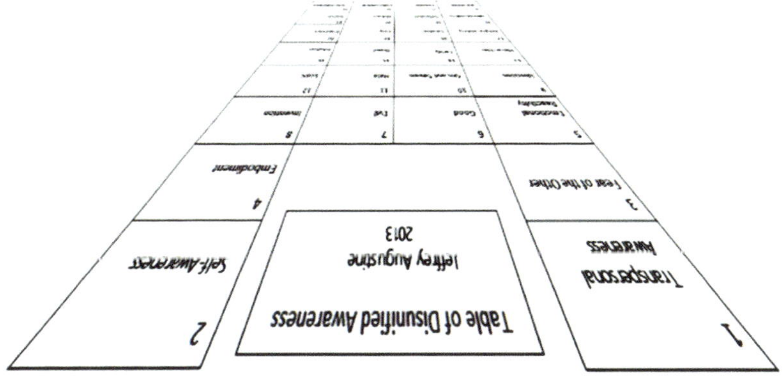

These images visually reinforce the conception that things were disunified and evolved in particular order in the Disunification.

DHARMAKAYA

The Buddhist term *Dharmakāya* wrestles with the origins and source of the Buddha and of all lesser Buddhas. From Wikipedia:

> The **Dharmakāya** (Sanskrit: धर्म काय; Pali: धम्म कय, lit. "truth body" or "reality body") is a central idea in Mahayana Buddhism forming part of the Trikaya doctrine that was possibly first expounded in the Aṣṭasāhasrikā prajñā-pāramitā (The Perfection of Insight In Eight Thousand Verses), composed in the 1st century BCE. It constitutes the unmanifested, "inconceivable" (Sanskrit: acintya) aspect of a Buddha, out of which Buddhas – and indeed all "phenomena" (Sanskrit: dharmas) – arise, and to which they return after their dissolution. Critical Buddhism argues that this concept is dhatu-vada (essentialist) and hence not Buddhist, because it posits that all things arise and return to an all-encompassing one[13].

Day Teaching explains why the unmanifested and inconceivable – which we call the Uncreate – disunifies Transpersonal Buddhas, Personal Divinities, angels, humans, demons, extraterrestrials, elementals, and all other identities.

Disunification Teaching explains why, "All things arise and return to an all-encompassing one."

The all-encompassing one is Infinity.

All things will eventually return to Infinity after a great journey.

---

[13] Retrieved online at: http://en.wikipedia.org/wiki/Dharmak%C4%81ya

KARMA

In Day Teaching, Karma means:

1. In its unified condition as One, Infinity cannot express Karma or any other separate thing. Karma is therefore a consequence of Disunification.

2. Karma is just another name for both the short and long term consequences of one's own actions. One can have either good karma, bad karma, or some form of intermediate karma. It all depends upon one's decisions, choices, and behavior. It is all on you.

3. Karma is created by one's own actions. To the extent that one acts based upon an identity, they reinforce the power and Karma of that identity. This strengthens the identity and drives a person deeper into an identity and further away from Consciousness.

4. As any identity strengthens, its predictive behaviors (or Karma) increase in proportion. One's Karma becomes one's future, fate, and destiny.

5. Because all identities are "psycho-synthetic forms" they all ultimately arise from the same Infinite Source Consciousness. However, as Consciousness disunifies, it differentiates into every possible identity that has ever existed or will ever exist.

6. All of the possible identities in our Universe are not predetermined. Rather, you as a sentient being choose from among all possibilities. Your destiny is what you chose relative to the range of possibilities available to you. Whatever possible identities you did not choose are realized in other dimensions or universe. Eventually, everyone realizes they are one person called Infinity. Hence, all possible histories and persons will be realized as a function of Disunification and not predestination. Predestination is the religious failure to comprehend Infinity in favor of a doctrinal model of God.

7. As you move away from Transpersonal Consciousness and into identity, your possibilities diminish with the square of the distance so to speak. Identities have far fewer possibilities available to them than does unfettered Transpersonal Consciousness.

8. At a certain threshold, an identity – which is psycho-synthetic in nature – "hardens" and flashes into a person's sense of Reality. While this sense of Reality is purely subjective, most people consider it to be objective.

9. Mistaking one's identity for Reality creates the Egoic condition in which the Ego is experienced as being alienated from others and the World itself. This in turns forces the individual to become defensive and to defend his or her Ego from all real or perceived external threats. Hence, one's negative Karmic liability increases as identity fuses into one's sense of Reality. One falls out of the moment of now and into the past or an imagined future.

10. Any identity shared by a group is inevitably converted by the group into a set of tautological and inflexible beliefs. At this level, Bad Karma intensifies when any group of people becomes radicalized and sets about to enforce their core identity and beliefs upon the World by use of violence.

DISUNIFIED AWARENESS AS TRANSPERSONAL ENLIGHTENMENT

I once had a realization that I, as disunified Awareness, could have been born into any time or place; been born male or female; spoken any language; and lived any life or any series of lives.

Time, place, gender, ethnicity, and everything else were only temporary states necessary to unfolding, evolving, and realizing my full potential across lifetimes. I am still in this process and will be for all Eternity.

I have literally experienced myself as being the transcendent, transpersonal Consciousness of the Universe in which all identities arise. I no longer needed to be myself or anyone else in particular, for I directly experienced the Root Consciousness of all temporal selves. And yet I am not God, for anyone can have the same transcendental realization. Moreover, "God" is just an identity.

Mine was an elegant realization born of years of spiritual practice and study. Those in disciplines such as Buddhism and Zen have had the same type of realization.

This realization is freely available to all. I simply arrived at it from a distinctly new point of view. My experience could be likened to climbing a very high mountain using a new approach and new gear.

I did not need either Eastern or Western religion to reach the summit. Rather, I made my own path to the top by walking it. What made my realization unique is that I discovered and then described the Disunification of Energy and Awareness.

I saw that that my particular life has an innate value, purpose, and destiny and that I had self-created these things as a function of my own Power.

You can do this too: You can declare who you are and what you will do as a function of your own Power.

THE UNFOLDING OF THE PRIMAL MATTER

I combined several of my images to create *The Unfolding of the Primal Matter.*

This image conveys my view that the physical Universe and Consciousness are inherently related and propagate in the seamless form of subject-object perception.

The Unfolding of the Primal Matter contains two groups of symbols placed at right angles to each other:

- ❖ The Periodic Table of the Elements and the dATable are overlaid upon each other and form the background of the image.

- ❖ In the foreground are the symbols that represent the Source Codes of Disunification and the Dream Tribe.

- ❖ The triangle in the corner represents the Source Codes and the Disunification

❖ The right angle placement of the Source Codes and the Dream Tribe to the two table evokes the image of electrons and magnetism propagating at right angles to form electromagnetism.

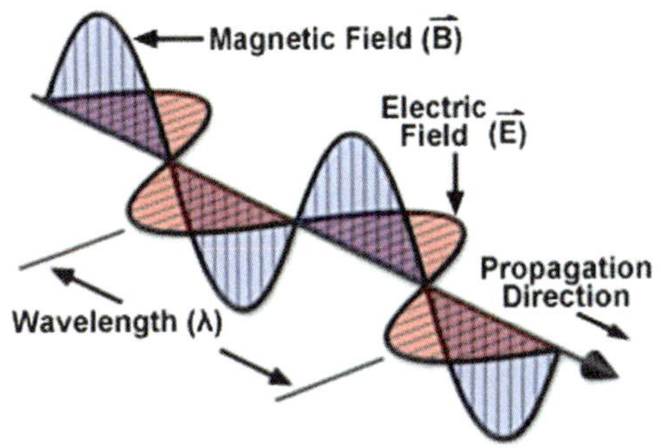

Electric and magnetic fields propagating as electricity.

Just as electricity is "made out of" the interaction of electrons and magnetism in motion, our Universe is made out of all of the interactions of disunified Energy and Awareness in motion.

At its highest level, this motion is called Consciousness.

Far below Consciousness are the "binding identities" of forms, processes, and beings.

These binding forms have been called "Maya" or an illusion in Eastern metaphysics.

Day Teaching reconceptualizes the concept of Maya by introducing the term ***Psycho-Synthetic Reality Process***.

The Psycho-Synthetic Reality Process is an intermediate of disunified existence.

Situated between the Primal Matter and Spiritual Enlightenment, this intermediate state contains great suffering.
To be free of this state is a matter of crucial importance. Material possessions and wealth cannot liberate people from the intermediate state. Only Spiritual Enlightenment can free you.

SECTION IV

THE CLOUD OF LIFE

The Cloud of Life

©Jeffrey Augustine

We have thus far answered two key questions:

- ❖ Who is God?
- ❖ How did the Universe begin?

The remainder of the book addresses the following central topics in terms of Day Teaching:

- ❖ How is the Hierarchy of Souls arranged in our Universe?
- ❖ Where are Heaven, Hell, the Bardo, and other spiritual states located?
- ❖ How do Souls come into existence?
- ❖ What is the nature and purpose of the Soul?
- ❖ How are the Soul and the Psyche related?
- ❖ Where happens when you die?
- ❖ Is the Universe an Illusion?

Chapter Nineteen

The Cloud of Life

© Jeffrey Augustine

THE CLOUD OF LIFE

The Cloud of Life image is akin to the Kabbalah's Tree of Life, in that it serves as a symbolic teaching device. However, Day Teaching is not Kabbalistic.

A multicolored field is the background for *The Cloud of Life*.

The multicolored field represents Transpersonal Consciousness as the background from out of which all living beings will arise and differentiate into the foreground of existence.

The multicolored background also represents disunified Awareness, with no identities in it.

This is pure Transpersonal Consciousness, pure Primal Matter, prior to any modifications.

Once the Cloud of Life was established following the Disunification, the Protogenoi, or early Divinities, began to condense out of the Cloud of Life and convert into Souls with Divine Identities.

Coincident with the Divinities converting from the Consciousness of the Cloud, the primeval majesty of the early physical Universe also began to convert from the Energy in the Cloud.

Accordingly, those Divinities who saw themselves reflected in the Power and the Glory of the early Universe identified themselves as the Creators of the Universe.

The Divinities and Matter are symbolized as colored diamonds.

Each of the colored diamonds below represents Divine beings and the naturalistic Universe.

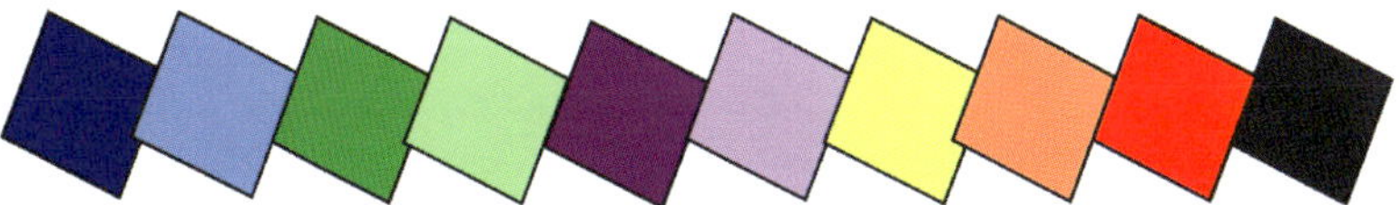

The Divinities and Matter are placed into the Cloud of Life to represent their having converted into "Big Souls" from out of the Cloud.

As Consciousness continued to disunify and expand, the next generation of angels, demons, higher intelligences, and other souls that condensed out of the Cloud of Life assumed their identities.

This second order is represented as smaller colored diamonds of different colors:

These smaller diamonds are added to the Cloud of Life.

Coincident with this second-level order, condensing out from the Cloud of Life, the **DNA Funnel** emerged as the **Biology Superhighway** that Disunification-Evolution needed to arise on life-friendly planets.

The DNA Funnel is the "silver cord that binds" Consciousness and Biology to form Intelligent Life:

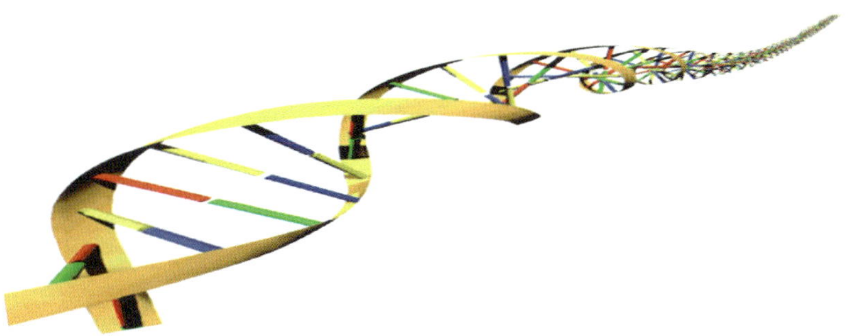

The DNA Funnel descends from the Cloud of Life.

After Disunification-Evolution established life on hospitable planets via the DNA Funnel, all manner of intelligent biological life (Consciousness entangled in Matter) appeared and evolved.

In the next image, human life, and all other forms of biological life are represented as a series of multicolored diamonds.

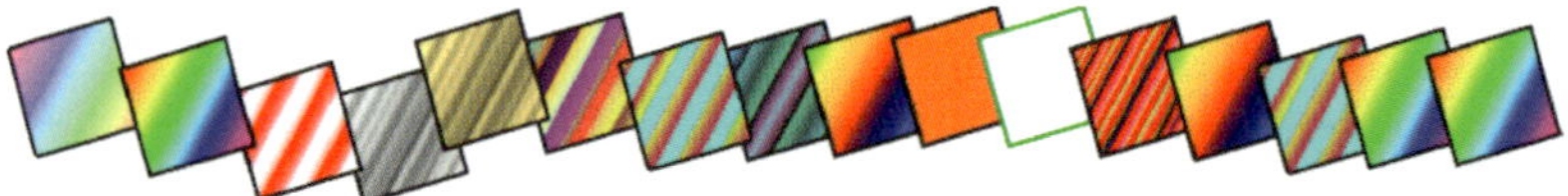

The image below shows Humanity – and all other forms of life on Earth – flowing from the Biology Superhighway. This Superhighway corresponds to the Multidimensional Superhighway that was used to unpackage our Universe.

Disunification-Evolution used the Biology Superhighway to transport the Primal Matter from the cold storage of Space to the warm terrestrial biological level.

Being an expression of Consciousness, human Souls naturally began to download and unpackage Primal Matter from the Cloud of Life.

This traffic is represented as a series of **three overlapping diamonds** (shown on the right side of the Cloud) interposed between the Divinities, Nature, and Humanity.

The pure and unhindered access to the Primal Matter Cloud is called a *Three Diamond State*, which speaks to the distinctive sense of having **Cloud Energy** flow through you. You are "in the zone" when you enter this state.

People who are passionately engaged in art, music, math, science, sports and every other field of endeavor experience all sorts of effortless energy and information flowing through them in the Three Diamond State. This state is inherently transformative as it allows people to make the jump from their previous levels of peak performance and understanding.

The common element in the Three Diamond State is profound concentration while involved in something about which we are passionate. Intense concentration and sole focus allow us unparalleled access to the Cloud and all that is contained therein.

In a pure Three Diamond State we become powerful agents of Disunification-Evolution as we unpackage the Primal Matter of Self and World with great ease, finesse, and skill – all of which occur as a function of our natural talents combined with years or decades of training and experience. You are literally at the Cutting Edge of Creation in this state.

Katsushika Hokusai's (1760-1849) internationally famous and instantly recognizable painting **The Great Wave off Kanagawa** is a dramatic image which symbolizes the Cutting Edge of Creation.

In the image, crews in boats ride the great wave. The crews are not overwhelmed; they are instead handling the wave with great skill. Mount Fuji is in the background to suggest the potential for greatness in everyday challenge and adversity.

POSTERITY

When you have children you pass on your DNA codes.

A second DNA Funnel is thus added to the bottom of the Cloud of Life to symbolize fertility and the posterity of biological life.

PSYCHO-MECHANICS:

GHOSTS, SPIRITS, AND ELEMENTALS

Ghosts, spirits, and elementals have long been a source of fascination and disturbance.

Ghosts are the souls, or "shades" of humans that have recently experienced a terrible death of one kind or another. Ghosts are often in an obsessive nightmare state in the Bardo.

"Spirit" is a colloquial term for many different types of non-human entities that include transdimensional beings, so-called shadow people, and familiar spirits.

"Elementals" are spiritual entities that are lower than humans.

As such, they are "Consciousness in fragmentary form" – i.e. they do not have a strong central identity as does a human.

Elementals are proto-egos that have a very weak sense of self.

Accordingly, they seek to attach themselves to available human Souls in order to experience a higher sense of self.

Once attached, these elementals seek to comingle themselves with their host's identity.

Ghosts, spirits, and elementals are entangled in human Souls and form part of the psychic traffic of the spiritual world.

These lower forms of fragmentary Consciousness are all traceable to the Disunification.

These forms of fragmentary Consciousness are still being disunified from the Primal Matter.

Nineteenth century American "Spiritualism" never understood any of this, nor did certain practitioners who sought to address the subject of elementals.

PSYCHO-MECHANICS:

EXTRATERRESTRIALS

Extraterrestrials are beings that come from other planets or dimensions using technologies that are, apparently, beyond present human comprehension.

Extraterrestrial conspiracies aside, the Drake Equation provides an ample statistical argument for the existence of intelligent life on other planets.

The Drake equation states that:

$$N = R^* \times f_p \times n_e \times f_l \times f_i \times f_c \times L$$

Where:

N is the number of civilizations in our galaxy that we might able to communicate with.

R^* is the average rate of star formation in our galaxy.

f_p is the fraction of those stars which have planets.

n_e is the number of planets that can support life.

f_l is the number of planets that develop intelligent life.

f_i is the civilizations that develop transmission technologies.

L is the length of time that these civilizations transmit their signals into space.

THE CLOUD OF LIFE COMPLETED

Ghosts, spirits, elementals, and extraterrestrials are symbolized as three rows of small multicolored diamonds:

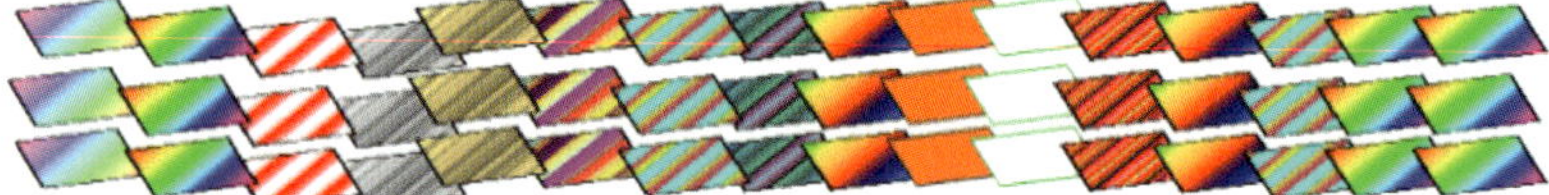

These three rows are added to the Cloud of Life to symbolize all other sentient forms of life known or unknown.

The Cloud of Life in its completed form.

The Levels in the Cloud of Life.

PSYCHO-MECHANICS:

REGIONS, STATES, AND ABSTRACTIONS

The Cloud of Life is vast and contains, among its vastness, the following Regions, States, and "Abstractions of Consciousness" described in classical spiritual literature:

- ❖ The Divinities, angels, demons, and all other nonphysical Sentient beings
- ❖ All Sentient physical beings
- ❖ All of the possible destinies for every person who has lived or will ever live
- ❖ Brahman
- ❖ Karma
- ❖ Archetypes and the Collective Unconscious
- ❖ The Bardo and other between-lives dimensions including Heavens and Hells
- ❖ The Akashic Records
- ❖ Plato's Forms
- ❖ Synchronicity
- ❖ The Muses

Everything is in the Cloud.

What you see depends upon who you are and where you are in the Cloud. Your observation, beliefs, identity, health, and State of Consciousness will bias what you see and experience in the Cloud of Life.

The unique psycho-mechanics and potent knowledge articulated in Day Teaching will greatly assist you in liberating yourself from the bondage to all forms of illusion. It will allow you to be free and ascend to ever higher levels in the Cloud of Life.

Chapter Twenty

HOW DOES THE SOUL COME INTO EXISTENCE?

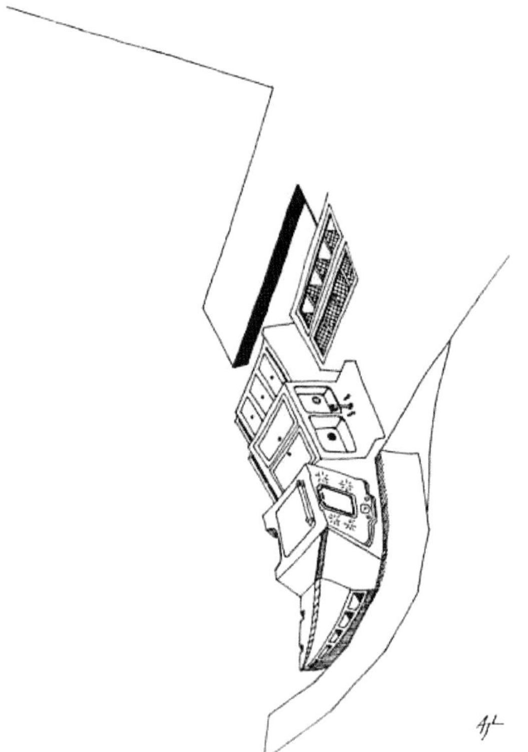

The Soul is Consciousness "knotted" into an Identity.

To say such a thing demands that we answer this question:

How does the Soul knot itself into existence in the first place?

We answer this question by using a piece of rope.

**Be it ever so humble,
There is no place like home.**

J. Augustine

THE SPECTRUM OF CONSCIOUSNESS

PART II

In terms of Consciousness, the definition of the word *Spectrum* is of vital interest.

"A spectrum is something that changes gradually and has no clear dividing points or lines, although its extremes are quite different. [14]"

The *Spectrum of Consciousness* is like a rope that goes on for eternity in both directions.

In this analogy, the opposite ends of the Spectrum would include Good and Evil and other contrasts that are normally considered opposites.

Such opposites are parts of a spectrum, or continuum, that goes on forever in our Universe:

If the Spectrum of Consciousness is like an endless piece of rope, then the Soul is a like a knot in that rope.

While a Soul is "made of" Consciousness, a Soul is nevertheless a very specific "binding modification" of Consciousness that summates to a Soul.

---

[14] Retrieved online at: http://vocabulary-vocabulary.com/dictionary/spectrum.php

Hence, a Soul is like a knot:

The figure-8 knot reminds us that Consciousness, when knotted into a Soul, bears a likeness of Infinity but is not Infinity.

An identity is Consciousness interrupted.

When a Soul knots itself into existence it gains individuation while simultaneously annihilating the pervasiveness it possessed as Consciousness.

A knot cannot be pervasive because it is a **Contraction of Consciousness**.

This is why while Consciousness pervades the Universe, Souls do not.

The logic of a knot is to remain tied, to remain bound.

Knots resist coming undone.

TYING YOURSELF INTO KNOTS

If Consciousness is sub-Infinite, then the Soul is even more so.

As Consciousness descends and knots itself into a Soul-in-a-body, it becomes entangled in the many definitions and limitations it assumes.

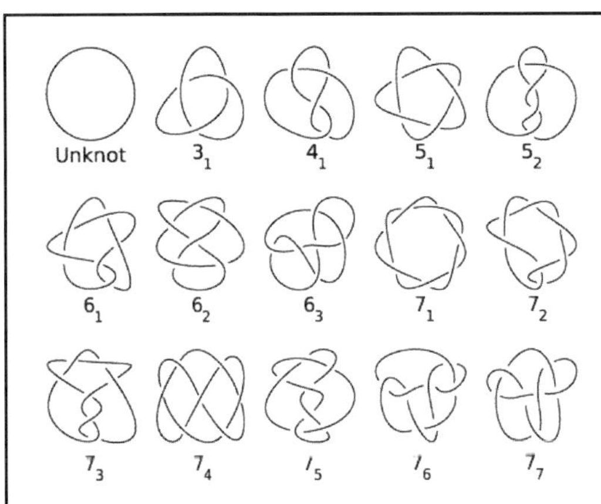

The Rolfsen Knot Table offers a visual metaphor for the endless permutations into which Souls can knot themselves.

Souls are sub-Infinite it is true.

However, Souls can and do knot themselves into endless permutations so that no two Souls are exactly alike.

This is physically reflected in human DNA and fingerprints.

Souls, like snowflakes, are complex patterns that resemble each other; however no two are alike.

The type and complexity of the knot, or identity, into which you as a Soul have knotted yourself is a reflection of your Karma.

THE SOUL AS A COMPOSITE BODY

Extending the visual analogy of the Soul as a piece of rope, we note that rope itself is braided out of many smaller strands, which are themselves braided from even smaller strings.

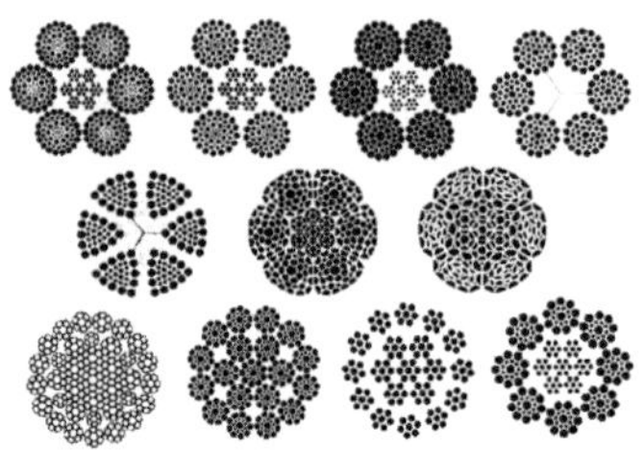

This industrial image shows cross section illustrations of modern metal rope designs.

The rope designs illustrate the complexity of the Soul as a "composite body" woven from the "elements" in the Periodic Table of disunified Awareness. It is worth noting, if only in passing, that these rope cross sections are evocative of mandalas.

The Soul is not one thing.

The Soul is not a self-contained, standalone, isolated, monolithic spiritual entity called "I."

If Souls were monolithic, they would only be composed of one thing and would thus have no inner conflict.

We all have some greater or lesser degree of inner conflict as our multifaceted and complex Souls unpackage into Life.

The sense of inner conflict you experience points to the fact that you are not monolithic but are rather a dynamic spectrum full of apparent polarities such as good and evil.

One thing you quickly learn doing any advanced form of spiritual work is that you, as a Soul, have many dynamic polarities and tensions within you.

Enlightenment is about noticing and expanding your range as Consciousness. Once you understand your range, the sense of polarities diminishes and the freedom to choose emerges.

CONSCIOUSNESS & THE EGO

True to the Myth of Narcissus, a new Soul wants to see its own reflection – it wants to see what it looks like.

Consequently, then, a new Soul travels through the **Realms of Disunified Phenomena** assaying the forms, processes, and beings it sees until it finds that which seems to mirror the Soul's image back to itself.

A new Soul thus identifies itself with those things which first mirror the Soul back to itself.

This primary act of identification binds the Soul to whatever disunified phenomena it considers to be itself.

The Soul's first "binding act of identification" is a **knot-creating Narcissus Experience**, for this type of experience transfixes the Soul into the reflection of its own image.

Narcissus is the Ego.

The Ego is a function of Disunification.

Karma and Ego are related inasmuch as the Soul is first attracted to that which resonates with its karmic pattern or image.

This is true across all lifetimes as the Soul is reborn over and over into situations that match its Karmic pattern and image.

Until a Karmic change occurs, no basic differences occur from lifetime to lifetime.

Ego can only fixate on its own image whereas Consciousness observes all things.

The Soul will remain Egoic until it spiritually awakens and begins to understand and realize its true nature, expanse, and the purpose of its own existence.

EXISTENTIALISM

The self-creation of Soul is the self-creation of identity.

As such, the self-creation of Soul is the first "existential" act and it begets all subsequent despair, angst, and bouts of meaninglessness.

Self-creation also begets the courage to find meaning in the face of nothingness.

By focusing on the Personal-Transpersonal nature of the Soul we can have our necessary transcendental abstractions and our indispensable personhood as well. We don't split our range.

While Day Teaching is not strictly existentialist, we are keenly aware that people can and do feel depersonalized or alienated by the World – and even by Disunification itself.

Paradoxically, these feelings of depersonalization and alienation are intensely personal feelings.

The Soul wrestles with its ***existential-disunified condition*** for, after having created itself, it must now create its own meaning and purpose.

When the Soul fails to accept responsibility for creating its own meaning and purpose it will fall into despair and meaninglessness.

In such a miserable condition, many Souls readily and eagerly accept a "plug and play identity system" as offered by religious, political, or other ideological causes.

Many people find it much easier to be told who they are and what to do rather than undertaking the very arduous work of discovering who they actually are.

What will you do?

Will you accept a plug and play identity system, or, will you find out who you really are?

EMBODIMENT

A wise Soul natively seeks to acquire as many "colors" as possible in order to become increasingly expressive, creative, and powerful. The colors a Soul acquires increase its vibrational level.

When a Soul attains a certain vibrational energy level it is pulled into the DNA funnel by the force of Disunification-Evolution and embodied into physical form.

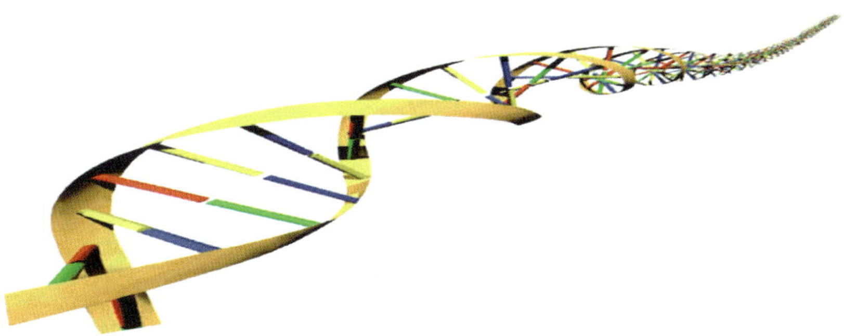

The type of physical body into which a Soul is pulled depends upon its level of Consciousness.

The concept of *Transmigration* is essentially correct: A Soul is first embodied in lower level bodies for orientation into the physical realm. The Soul then transmigrates up into a human body.

The Soul is then reborn into a long succession of human bodies until it transcends the human condition.

Transcending the human condition does not necessarily mean that one is liberated from the wheel of birth and death altogether. Rather, one is liberated from rebirth into the human condition.

The human body is not the highest level of physical body. There are other worlds where bodies live for hundreds or thousands of years or longer.

However, the Souls inhabiting those types of bodies are of a much higher level of Consciousness. They acquired virtue, good Karma, and sufficient enlightenment to raise their Soul Energy above the human level.

Humans are at a transitional juncture in Consciousness.

You are either expanding or contracting at the human level.

Human life truly is a "School of the Spirits."

There is no standing still here: You are either expanding your Consciousness or you are contracting it.

Disunification-Evolution and Karma are thus understood as an interlocking system in which one's Soul Energy is "frequency matched" to a corresponding type of life:

❖ A Soul creates and amasses its own Karma, or Soul energy, by virtue of its own self-creation and subsequent conduct.

❖ Goodness increases Soul Energy. Goodness is inherently constructive, positive, and life-affirming. If you are constructive, positive, and life-affirming, then you are a Good person.

❖ Evil degrades Soul Energy. The basic thing to know about Evil is that it is inherently and always deliberately harmful and destructive. Evil destroys self and others. If what you are doing, or tending to do, is deliberately destructive to yourself or others, then it is Evil. Some things are more Evil than others, but still, Evil is Evil and bears a poisonous fruit.

❖ Disunification-Evolution incarnates Souls into bodies based upon their Karma, or Soul Energy. To reincarnate to a higher level requires that one increase their Good Karma through virtuous conduct. This is just how it is in our Universe.

KARMIC LAYERING

The light bodies, or collective energies in your Soul, are "karmically layered" to either attenuate or amplify the Soul's energy and purposes.

You always have the power to change your Karma by changing your behavior.

Hence, you can literally change your own Soul by choosing to behave virtuously.

If you are essentially Evil, your karmically layering attenuates, or seriously restricts, your Soul's natural flow of Life Energy.

As you persist in Evil, your Soul goes darker and darker as its inner light bodies, or energies, die off.

When a person commits a very Evil act it is not uncommon for them to say that something in them has died.

This sense of an inner death is a warning to the Soul that it is going downwards towards destruction and perdition.

This sense of an inner death is an accurate intuition, for what has died within is an essential part of who they are. What has died is a light body, a part of the very energy of their Soul.

Evil destroys the Soul.

Specifically, Evil crushes and warps the Soul into the state of being a nonhuman monster, i.e. a sadistic, disfigured, murderous criminal.

At death, Evil people are brutally punished in the Bardo and then transmigrated down into the Hell Worlds.

People can scoff at the idea of Hell but it does not change their Karma or what happens in the Bardo.

If you are basically Good then your karmic layering amplifies your Soul's natural flow of Life Energy.

As you persist in Good, your Soul becomes brighter and brighter.

It is not uncommon for a person on a Good path to realize that some new sense of purpose or aliveness is being born within them.

This is an accurate intuition, for a new light body, a new vital energy level, is emerging within the Soul by virtue of attaining good karma.

This sense of an inner birth is a confirmation to the Soul that it is continuing its ascent towards higher states.

Day Teaching is very Classical and Old World in maintaining that the deeds done in this life are either rewarded or punished in the Afterlife and also affect one's future incarnations.

Day Teaching differs from the old "Judgmental God" religions by identifying Transpersonal Karma as the Agent of Consciousness that always acts to balance energy flows within Consciousness.

A Judgmental God is not needed when Transpersonal Karma always inexorably acts to balance energy flows as a function of Disunification-Evolution.

Good forwards the progress of Disunification-Evolution and is rewarded in many ways with increased survival, health, fitness, and strength.

Evil destroys the progress of Disunification-Evolution and is punished with destruction and death.

What happens after death is explained in chapter thirty.

Chapter Twenty-One

Colorized Version of the Flammarion Woodcut
Artist Unknown, Circa 1880

THE UNCONSCIOUS REDEFINED

One of the problematic areas of the human personality is what Sigmund Freud called the Unconscious. The website About.com offers a very simple definition of the Unconscious as articulated by Freud:

> "In Freud's psychoanalytic theory of personality, the unconscious mind is a reservoir of feelings, thoughts, urges, and memories outside of our conscious awareness. Most of the contents of the unconscious are unacceptable

or unpleasant, such as feelings of pain, anxiety, or conflict. According to Freud, the unconscious continues to influence our behavior and experience, even though we are unaware of these underlying influences."[15]

An iceberg has been used as a metaphor to illustrate Freud's model in which most psychological content is repressed and therefore "stored" in the Unconscious.

Freud's discovery of the Unconscious was a remarkable one in its day, for it allowed people to think about and discuss repressed psychological content.

Day Teaching redefines Freud's concept of the Unconscious altogether.

When Consciousness knots, or converts, into an identity, that identity prevents almost the entire Spectrum of Consciousness from being expressed.

---

[15] Retrieved online at:
http://psychology.about.com/od/uindex/g/def_unconscious.htm

This is because an identity is most fundamentally a limitation, or contraction, of Consciousness.

The Spectrum of Consciousness does not simply disappear because an identity has come into existence. Rather, an identity can only exist as such by denying and repressing a large part of the Spectrum of Consciousness.

This repressed region of Consciousness becomes, by default, the Unconscious.

It is very important to carefully differentiate between the Unconscious and physical unconsciousness.

To be physically unconscious – as happens when one goes under anesthesia or is knocked unconscious in an accident – is quite different from the Unconscious.

While one can be fully conscious as their identity, they can also simultaneously be "Unconscious" relative to the larger Spectrum of Consciousness in which they arise.

The Spectrum of Consciousness is transpersonal, unstructured, amorphous, and pervasive. Conversely, an identity is highly focused upon itself.

To the degree that the Soul is self-focused, or self-centered., it is excluded from seeing, or consciously participating in the larger Spectrum of Consciousness.

When the Soul knots itself into existence, it becomes blind, or unconscious, to the ***larger Spectrum of Consciousness*** out of which it has knotted itself.

The Spectrum of Consciousness is the background to the Cloud of Life.

All of the Souls, or identities, in the Universe are foreground objects in the Cloud of Life.

All souls are contractions, or knots, within Consciousness.

The ***Unconscious*** is the part of the Spectrum of Consciousness that is ordinarily quite unavailable to the Soul.

The following pages expand upon the redefinition of the Unconscious to include the Stream of Consciousness and the Unconsciousness as Unwanted Psychoactive Content.

THE STREAM OF CONSCIOUSNESS

The Cloud of Life is heavily laden with the Primal Matter – the very essence of Life.

Being so heavily laden, the Cloud of Life relentlessly rains down the Primal Matter upon everything and everyone.

The Cloud of Life rains down Primal Matter especially hard into the towering and rugged peaks of the human mind and imagination.

All of this Primal Matter from the Cloud of Life runs down the towering and rugged peaks to feed a mighty and ancient Stream that has always – and will always – course through all Souls forever.

This Stream is the fabled **Stream of Consciousness**. It is the Primal Matter – driven by the force of Disunification-Evolution – ceaselessly unpackaging intense psychoactive content into the Souls of all sentient beings in our Universe.

The "Stream of Consciousness" is a beautifully descriptive term to describe the process of the Primal Matter unpackaging itself within all Souls.

When potent psychoactive content enters the Soul via the Stream of Consciousness, such content can in fact seem like uncontrollable, troubling, and unwanted feelings, images, and sensations emerging from the Unconscious.

This type of content and occurrence is the Primal Matter unpackaging within your very Soul.

What can make this highly natural psychoactive process so troubling is that the Primal Matter does not need your permission to unpackage itself within your Soul.

Indeed, the Primal Matter does not need your permission to unpackage itself within your Soul any more than a thunderstorm needs your permission to pour down lighting and torrential rain upon your head.

The Primal Matter can be spoken of as the psychic weather traveling through your head. You are not responsible for the weather, and yet you have to be very aware of it and learn how to allow it to pass without harming you.

THE UNCONSCIOUS

Why does the Unconscious arise?

It arises because the conventional forms of identity established by religion, parents, and culture create rigid definitions of who you must be and who you cannot be. Thus, identity becomes an arbitrary limitation of the full Spectrum of Consciousness.

The pervasive identity that most people are trying to be is what is called a **Good Person**.

Add to this the perfectionist tendencies inherit in so many of us and what so many of us are trying to be is a **Good Person who is Perfect**.

Instead of acknowledging the full Spectrum of Consciousness, almost everyone is taught in childhood to be a good person, to obey rules, and to only have and think good thoughts.

Many children are also taught that they must be perfect. The instruction to be a good person is often accompanied by discipline and punishment when one has not been a good person or has expressed evil thoughts. Praise is usually given when one has been a Good Person.

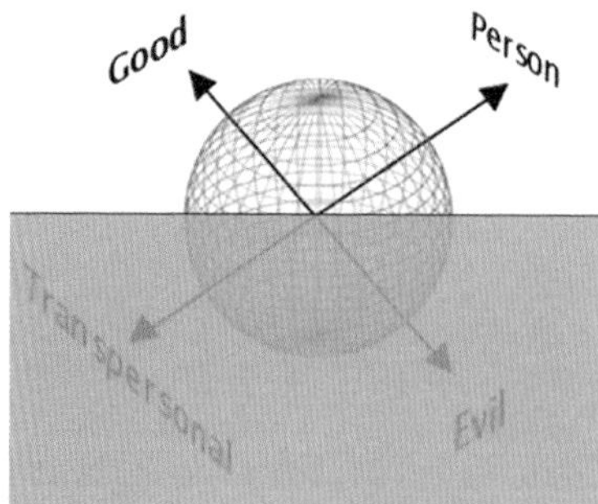

In some families, any misbehavior is handled with violent and traumatic verbal or physical abuse.

The net effect of such discipline and punishments is to cause a child to suppress half of their Consciousness, or more, in order to be a good person.

Granted, the definition of a "good person" differs among families, religions, and cultures. The point is that a "good person" is an identity that requires a person to suppress or "gray out" a large part of their own Consciousness as shown in the illustration.

When this suppressed region of Consciousness is denounced as forbidden, taboo, or even demonic, a person splits it off from himself or herself. This entire region of Consciousness thus becomes a person's Unconscious. It is extremely unwise to leave this much of yourself unavailable, unexplored, unacknowledged, and unexamined.

SEXUALITY AND THE UNCONSCIOUS

The Bible long ago pronounced the entire human condition to be Evil and unregenerate. This denunciation is both cruel and untrue.

The power of conventional religion is the fact that God is present

To be biblically religious, therefore, is to be in a perpetual and unwinnable state of war with one's own Existence and Consciousness.

This war is made worse by the arbitrary moral pronouncements of the Bible and other Scriptures.

For example, the Bible teaches that men are to be manly and domineering and that women are to be demure, quiet, and submissive to their husbands. However, a four corner diagram reveals part of the actual range of Consciousness in all of us.

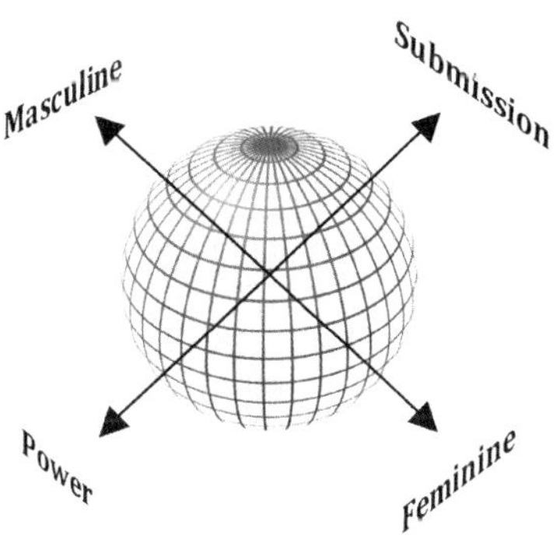

Fixed religious gender roles require men to be masculine and women to be submissive and feminine. Under this scheme, feminine men and powerful women are Evil and are to be

despised and punished until and unless they repent and change their ways.

This sounds shockingly simplistic and judgmental and yet it is true: Religion demands that people adopt very rigid and defined gender roles while denouncing the nonreligious who refuse to adopt religious gender roles. Religion is based upon an enforced identity called **A Good Person who serves God and fights Evil.**

Due to the very limited nature of religious morality, human sexuality very much interferes with trying to be a good person who serves God.

The Bible condemns gay, lesbian, bisexual, and transgendered ("GLBT") people as Evil.

Religious people fight and condemn GLBT people every day. Therefore, in order to be a "Good Person who serves God and fights Evil," Christians, Mormons, Muslims, and many other religious people are obligated to fight GLBT people and denounce them as Evil.

Many religious people take great delight in condemning and hating others as it makes them feel better about themselves and their own identity. This does not say much about them.

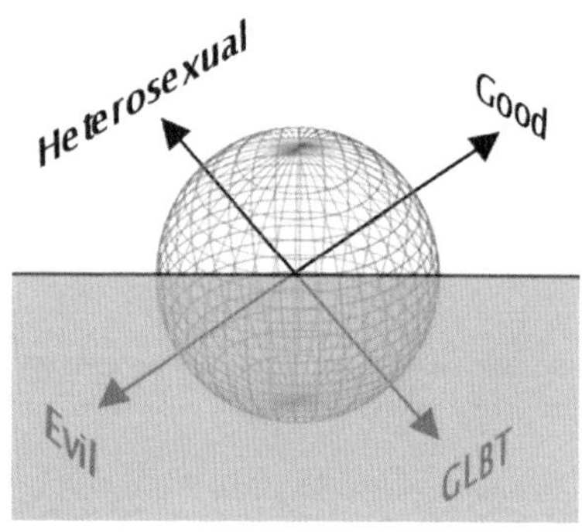

However, many religious people also have sexual feelings and needs that exist at a repressed and somewhat unconscious level.

Religious repression sets the stage whereby religious people develop secret sexual lives.

This invariably all falls apart when they are caught and pilloried as hypocrites.

There really is no need for religious people to be ruined in this way when they can simply leave religious life and stop living a lie.

Religious people, particularly Christians and Muslims, strive to be an identity called **Good Heterosexuals**. This is a subset of their larger identity called **A Good Person who serves God and fights Evil.**

As a consequence of these identities, such religious people prejudicially denounce all other forms of sexuality as "Evil." They are blind to the fact that labels such as heterosexual, gay, lesbian, bisexual, and transgendered are all simply part of the vast expanse of human sexuality and Consciousness. Religious people are rightfully seen as judgmental bigots when they attack others based upon their very narrow and biased view of human Consciousness.

LAW & ORDER

The real issue is not sexual preference but rather sexual conduct. Sexual conduct of any kind that is criminal in nature – such as rape or child molestation – is demonstrably evil and needs to be severely punished. One does not need any religious book to tell them that certain forms of sexual conduct are Evil and that evildoers must be dealt with in the most severe of terms.

The fact that human Consciousness has a vast expanse does not excuse Evil in any way whatsoever. Rather, the vast expanse of human Consciousness must draw our attention to the need to establish and maintain a strong justice system in order to keep Evil in check. This is really no different than building a series of flood control channels to control a wild rampaging river that swells during storms and has the power to destroy entire cities by flooding.

Recognizing and controlling Evil is an inescapable necessity in disunified Life. Justice must exist to protect law-abiding citizens from criminals and terrorists. The "gray areas" in Justice are parts of the Spectrum of Consciousness where criminality blends into disgraceful behavior that, while not technically illegal, is nevertheless morally inexcusable and destructive.

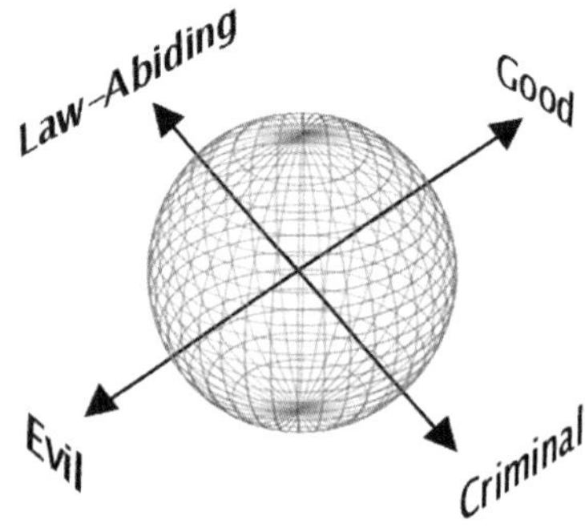

For the common good and order, Society has a vested interest in a communal identity called ***Good Law-Abiding Citizens.***

In this case, the citizenry itself decides what the laws shall be. Laws should never be solely determined based upon religious books and religious people.

While religious sensibilities should play a role in any Culture, when religious sensibilities warp over into Fascism, they must be opposed.

The struggle between opposing forces in Culture is a part of the unpackaging pressure of Disunification-Evolution. As any Culture moves into the future, it can and will challenge the older religious rules and customs that had previously defined what were **allowed identities** and what were **disallowed identities**.

Based upon the power and vast sweep of the Internet, it is clear to see that human Consciousness is demanding for itself more allowed identities and freedom than at any previous time in human history.

This demand has to be balanced within the legal framework so that criminals do not run rampant. We also do not want governmental, corporate, or financial fascists to run rampant either.

The Free People of the World are presently on a collision course with criminals and fascists who seek to control the wealth and resources of the planet.

The next unprecedented phase of Disunification-Evolution will be about two things: The collapse of Religion and, the war between the People and Government-Corporate fascists and surveillance. Revolution is a bloody aspect of Disunification in which pent up energies are released in asymmetrical ways that corrupt Establishments have a hard time fighting.

SELF RIGHT/OTHERS WRONG

Many other types of four corner diagrams can be made to illustrate the point that identities are suffocating when they arbitrarily split off some part of any person's full Consciousness.

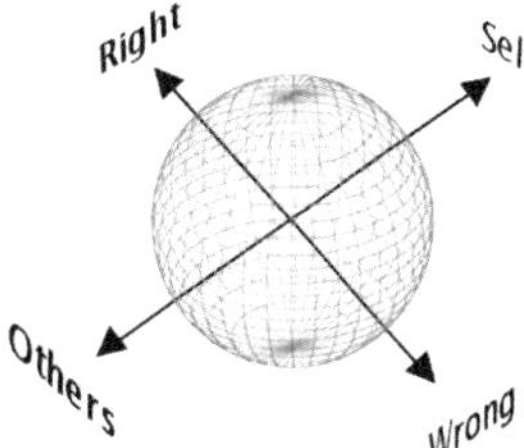

As a general statement, most identities are reactively based upon making one's self right and others wrong. And yet, even the distinctions of "Self and Other" and "Right and Wrong" are also part of the full range of Consciousness.

To operate based upon the logic "I am right and others are wrong" is to contract one's own Consciousness into a defensive and emotionally reactive identity. Add to this the repression or denial of other parts of one's Consciousness and the result is a very narrow-minded and bigoted fundamentalist identity.

Fundamentalists come in all stripes.

You don't even need religion to be a fundamentalist; you just need to be intolerant and ignorant.

To be spiritually liberated is to expand beyond your own intolerance and ignorance.

MAKE YOUR OWN DIAGRAMS

You can make your own four corner diagrams to examine any hurtful form of identity arising within you.

Instructions to do four corner diagrams:

- ❖ Notice what identity you are trying to be and then notice its opposite
- ❖ Notice why you are trying to be that particular identity
- ❖ Notice what part of Consciousness you must split off, deny, or pronounce as Evil in order to defend that identity
- ❖ Note the costs as well as the losses incurred in being that particular identity

The goal of recognizing and dismantling harmful identities is to liberate one's self into the full Spectrum of Consciousness.

To the degree that one is Unconscious, they are blind.

Anyone can open their eyes any time they want.

The key principle is this: Realize that you are ultimately not your identity or any identity.

Realize that you arise as Consciousness.

We have much more to say on this matter.

UNWANTED PSYCHOACTIVE CONTENT

Even after one achieves full Consciousness, unwanted content still arises from within.

What does one do with unwanted content?

Jung teaches that any unconscious content we reject will manifest symptomatically in harmful ways. That which we reject in ourselves must be taken back, accepted, and integrated into Soul if we are to find balance and adjustment according to the argument of the Jungians.

Day Teaching takes a different view. We see unwanted content entering the Soul in terms of Disunification-Evolution.

Primal Matter is unpackaging itself in and through you all the time. You are one of the portals through which the Primal Matter enters the Universe.

Some of the Primal Matter is irrational because it contains illogical fragments of Infinity. It is **detritus**:

> **detritus /de tri tus/ (de-tri′tus) particulate matter produced by or remaining after the wearing away or disintegration of a substance or tissue.**

You do not have to accept any Primal Matter content you do not want to keep. You just look at it, acknowledge it, and then watch it vanish as it exits into the Universe.

It is like this: If the Sky opened up and a big thunderstorm washed up some mud on your front porch, you would shovel the mud back into the field from whence it came.

You do not have to keep the mud or do anything about it.

On the other hand, if a thunderstorm washed up some gold nuggets onto your front porch, you would of course keep those.

The Cloud of Life is a big ongoing thunderstorm that feeds the Stream of Consciousness.

The Stream of Consciousness brings mud and gold and everything in between. Keep what you want and let the rest pass into the Universe for recycling. You did your part by unpackaging it and releasing it back into the Stream. Someone somewhere else will find a use for it. Nothing is wasted.

When you refuse to acknowledge Stream content by repressing it, you build a psychological dam against its natural flow.

This backed-up content builds up pressure in your Soul. This pent-up energy will eventually break down your psychological dam.

To the degree that you do not identify yourself with the content from the Stream of Consciousness, you can allow all Cloud content to enter and pass harmlessly through your Soul.

You only have to keep that which pertains to you.

You do not have to repress anything if you can merely observe it and allow it to pass through and disunify itself into the World.

SPIRITUAL ENLIGHTENMENT

The reason it is important to understand the Unconscious is because we want to make it fully conscious so that its negative effects disappear. You cannot make something disappear unless you know it is there in the first place.

In Day Teaching, spiritual enlightenment is about expanding the personal and collective bandwidth of humanity so that all of us can continually overcome and transcend the barriers in the human condition.

We want to expand the personal and collective bandwidth of humanity into a much broader region of the Spectrum of Consciousness.

We want to expand people as close as possible to Infinity by eliminating as much of the Unconscious as possible.

As we become more enlightened, more and more Unconsciousness and its attendant pain and violence will disappear.

On the individual and collective level, we must overcome all of our technological, spiritual, financial, psychological, relational, genetic, and other barriers. We can only do this by removing all barriers. We can best remove barriers by becoming Fully Conscious.

EXPANDING YOUR CONSCIOUSNESS

This book focuses on dismantling the ancient religious and spiritual barriers by using Day Teaching to take them apart at a very fundamental level.

As you expand your Consciousness, you will naturally become increasingly sensitive, spiritual, moral, and powerful. Some people will become materially prosperous as a result of Spiritual Enlightenment while others find they want as little as possible to do with Materialism and so take vows of poverty.

I respect both outcomes as well as intermediate outcomes. I tend to travel right down the middle of things; the Great Middle Path is full of wisdom and generosity. The fact is that the Soul is in no way bound to any ancient and unworkable religious rules or codes.

We as a race must personally and collectively locate, unpackage, and articulate new rules and codes from within our own emerging Primal Matter. We alone contain all the answers we need; we just need to find and unpackage those answers.

We can look within the Primal Matter that is contained in our incredibly rich and vast intelligence and imagination. Sometimes our future self that is not yet unpackaged will speak to us when we seek answers. The voice of our future self sometimes seems like Destiny, but it is actually who we are meant to become.

We have to "think ahead" of current predicaments and bring forth a new future. All of the answers are contained in the Cloud of Life in which we arise, appear, and have our being. But the journey is long and there is so much Primal Matter yet to unpackage.

We are all babes in this Universe. We still have a long way to go.

With this in mind, the next section will look back at the creation myths and religions of the World to see how these things unpackaged and evolved from the Primal Matter of Consciousness. We will also explore how creation myths and religions are now falling apart under the inexorable onslaught of Disunification-Evolution.

SECTION V

THE DIVINITIES

Moses, Michelangelo

In the next chapter we begin a discussion of the Personal and Transpersonal Divinities in terms of Day Teaching.

We take religious and spiritual people at their word and acknowledge that Divinities, angels, demons, and many other different types of spirits and intelligences exist in our Universe and interact with humans. This type of communion has gone on forever.

The Divinities are real to billions of people and the objections of secular people mean little or nothing at all.

People believe in various Gods and experience a Divine presence on a daily basis.

There is something to all of this.

Chapter Twenty-Two

STRANGE NATURE:

THE DIVINITIES

My work is simple.

I open Pandora's Box.

The Disunification is Pandora's Box.

From out of Pandora's Box flies a Universe full of colors, emotions, wavelengths, particles, forces, and people. Aquamarine ultraviolet gravity chases charmed quarks across Einstein's front yard. Einstein yells at the quarks to keep off his yard, but they remain a constant problem he may yet solve.

Our situation is evident: We are limited beings arising within a situation that seldom makes sense.

Why should it make sense? This is a Special Dream and these kinds of dreams seldom make sense.

You see, this place is exactly what LELA desired.

Our World is a potent, ferocious, mysterious, paradoxical, sensual realm that is completely free of the limitations of Infinity.

Look around you: there is no Unity here.

What exists is Tension, Evolution, Struggle and all of the consequences that go with the demands of survival within Disunification.

Ours is an existential situation full of the tortured contradictions of order and chaos, love and hate, wealth and poverty, and all the rest.

Where else could Michelangelo sculpt desire; granite high rises overshadow slum children; Minister Jones and his nine hundred drink poison Kool-Aid in the jungle and die; or God be disunified?

My purpose is bold.

I dethrone Religion as the holder of God's Scepter. No one holds God's Scepter in this Universe – not Science, not you, and certainly not me. I would not be God for all of the money and power in the World.

My teaching is direct: Infinity disunifies Universes, Physics, Divinities, Humans, Religion and everything else.

As we say, forms, processes, and beings.

DIVINITIES DIVIDED

During the Disunification, the Dream Tribe members were separated from each other and rendered sub-Infinite.

Some of the Dream Tribe disunified into Personal Divinities whereas others disunified into Transpersonal Divinities or Archetypes.

Divinities and Archetypes alike express some aspect of disunified Consciousness.

At the top of the human religious hierarchy sit certain Dream Tribe members whose power as Divinities increased by virtue of human acclamation and worship.

These are the **Power Deities** who interact with certain humans to create religions.

The diagram below shows how certain Dream Tribe members disunified into the two basic divine forms:

Dream Tribe Members

↓

Disunification

↓

Sub-Infinite Divinities

↙ ↘

Personal Divinities   Transpersonal Divinities

THE DIVINE GNOSIS IS FRAGMENTARY

Because they helped to initiate the event, the Disunification did not exist for those Dream Tribe members who became Divinities. Rather, they experienced themselves as having spontaneously flashed into pure, elemental existence in our Universe in the Great Light and Thunderclap.

Relative to our Universe, then, nothing existed before they did.

These Divinities were never born. They saw themselves as existing over against the Chaos of Nature and considered that they were superior in every way to the primitive, chaotic gas clouds that filled the early Universe. These exalted beings are the self-created **Disunification Divinities**.

The **Ancient Egyptian Book of the Dead** says something that is powerfully explained by Day Teaching:

> **"I stand before the masters who witnessed the genesis, who were the authors of their own forms, who walked the dark, circuitous passages of their own becoming."**[16]

This ancient observation is perfectly understood in terms of Day Teaching, for these Disunification Divinities indeed witnessed the genesis.

They considered that they were the "uncreated authors" of their own forms because they were.

---

[16] **Ancient Egyptian Book of the Dead**. Normandi Ellis translation.

THE ZEP TEPI

The Dream Tribe members walked the "dark, circuitous passages of their own becoming" in the Day Dream Pyramid, the Disunification, and in the blackness of the early Universe.

The term **"Zep Tepi"** comes from Book of the Dead and means the "first time." From the perspective of Day Teaching, there are numerous creation mythologies because there are numerous Divinities that crossed over in the Disunification.

As such, they communicated their respective points of view about what they saw and experienced in the Zep Tepi.

The Divinities who emerged from the Disunification were completely free to make certain grand and cosmic conclusions.

These conclusions would depend upon both the nature of their essence and what they could recall about Infinity and the Disunification.

Once the One in Infinity became the Many in Disunity, there were suddenly many Divinities. This created the original War in Heaven, a tension of polarities that has never ended.

Creation mythologies abound because Divinities abound. As we have seen, there were many Divinities who saw and experienced the Beginning. They indeed emerged from the Disunification as the uncreated authors of their own forms.

None of these Divinities were born. However, like everyone else in this Universe, they preexisted in Infinity and were disunified. When they passed through Disunification they were rendered sub-Infinite.

Accordingly, the ***Infinite Gnosis*** was disunified into countless fragmentary views. Specifically, part of the Infinite Gnosis was disunified into the separate Personal Consciousness of every Sentient Being who has ever lived or ever will live.

We all have some pieces of Infinity within us. When we add up the sum total of collective Humanity, we see a much larger piece of Infinity than any individual can affords us.

The diagram below shows how the **Disunification** itself spawned the two basic Eastern and Western forms of religious identity.

<table>
<tr><td>

Transpersonal Consciousness Religions

Characteristics:

- **Transpersonal Divine Energies**

- **Search for Truth**

- **Eastern Philosophy**
- **Non-Duality**
- **Physical Universe is an Illusion**
- **Human Identity is Illusion**
- **Seeks Liberation from Illusion**
- **Karma**
- **Reincarnation**

</td><td>

Personal Consciousness Religions

Characteristics:

- **A Personal God and Salvation**

- **Search for the "One True God"**

- **Western Theology**
- **Duality**
- **Physical Universe Created by God**
- **Human Identity is Real**
- **Seeks Salvation from Sin and Evil**
- **God's Judgment**
- **Live only one life**

</td></tr>
</table>

Combined religious forms such as Hinduism, Pantheism, etc. in which Personal and Transpersonal Divine Energies are combined.

The chief attribute of Personal Divinities is ***Immanence***.

As we use the term, Immanence is the ability of Personal Divinities to pervade human Consciousness and to commune and interact with humans.

To pervade some fragmentary part of human Consciousness, i.e. the Souls of believers, is not the same thing as pervading the Universe. Hence, the Personal Divinities do not pervade the Universe.

Conversely, there are Transpersonal, or Abstract Divine Energies.

These forms of Transpersonal Consciousness have variously been described as Brahman, Atman, Oversoul, and so forth.

The chief attribute of this class of Transpersonal Energies is Transcendence.

As we use the term, Transcendence is the ability to pervade some part of human Consciousness without needing an Identity to do so.

A Transpersonal Divinity can exert a particular type of influence or energy that has no central identity.

In this sense, Transpersonal Divinities and Archetypes are synonymous.

As a general rule, Personal Divinities need and require the structure of language, i.e. they communicate in and through Scripture.

Personal Divinities also need the energy offered up by human praise. Thus it is written in the Psalm, "God inhabits the praises of his people."

On the other hand, Transpersonal Divinities understand that language falsifies transcendental experience and understanding.

Hence, the Transpersonal Divinities place emphasis on the direct experience beyond words and language.

THE DOMAINS OF DIVINE PSYCHOACTIVITY

We teach that religious people commune with actual Divine Persons.

Those who have never experienced deep spiritual communion with a Divinity are locked out of the massive ***Domains of Divine Psychoactivity*** offered by the Divinities.

My term, the Domain of Divine Psychoactivity means exactly what it says: The Divinities are Psychoactive, and, humans have accessed these domains since time immemorial. These domains are always open to humans.

The Domain of Divine Psychoactivity exists in the Spectrum of Consciousness.

To gain entrance requires one to surrender their Free Consciousness and be converted into the image and likeness of their Divinity.

This imperfect conversion is full of tears; it is the Via Dolorosa.

THE DISUNIFICATION PANTHEON

Who were the first Divinities to appear in our Universe?

In Greek mythology, they were called the ***Protogenoi***. From the Greek, the word Protogenoi refers to the primeval Gods and Goddesses who were the "firstborn" at the very beginning of the Universe. Ai Mystai says of the Protogenoi:

> "...The Protogenoi were the first entities or beings that came into existence whose forms made up the very fabric of our universe and they were immortal. The name singular is Prôtogenos and in plural Prôtogenoi and both mean as First Born of Primeval. The Prôtogenoi are group of Gods from which all the other Gods are descended from. Although it is believed that they were the first Gods who came out of the Void or Chaos, some sources mentioned a pair of deities who were the parents of these Prôtogenoi. These deities represent various elements of nature like Water (Pontos), Earth (Gaia), Heaven (Ouranos), etc... There were even Prôtogenos of the Seas (Pontos), Islands (Nesoi), Air (Khaos), Mists of Light (Aither), Day (Hemera), Mists of Darkness (Erebos), Procreation (Himeros- Eros), Mountains (Ouranoi), Sea surface (Thalassa), Ocean (Okeanos), the great stormy Hellpit (Tartarus which was seen as both a deity and the personification), Creation (Thesis) and Fresh Water (Thetis). These are the names who made up the Prôtogenoi..."[17]

In terms of Disunification Spirituality, it would be quite natural for those Divinities, or Higher Intelligences, that desired to commune with early humans to associate themselves with the parts of Nature vital to human existence. These "Communion Divinities" could easily localize some part of their Spiritual Energy in bodies of water, gardens, pastures, fruit trees, animals, groves, wells, and other important places.

---

[17] Retrieved online at http://ai-mystai.faithweb.com/protogenoi.html

Who inhabits the Pantheon of Disunification?

Judged by the number of their followers - and the power and wealth of their followers - the big "A List" Divinities include YHWH, Jesus, Allah, Buddha, and Krishna.

The website Adherents.com ranked the most populous world religions in 2012.[18] The top ten are:

1. Christianity: 2.1 billion

2. Islam: 1.5 billion

3. Secular/Nonreligious/Agnostic/Atheist: 1.1 billion

4. Hinduism: 900 million

5. Chinese traditional religion: 394 million

6. Buddhism: 376 million

7. Primal-Indigenous: 300 million

8. African Traditional & Diasporic: 100 million

9. Sikhism: 23 million

10. Juche: 19 million

What stands out in this list is the fact that "Personal Consciousness" religions are much larger than "Transpersonal Consciousness" religions.

The reason is that Personal Divinities offer people simple *plug and play identity systems*. These plug and play religious identity systems offer apparent answers to the basic questions of Life.

These systems do not require the hard work of meditation and inquiry demanded by Transpersonal systems, such as Buddhism, wherein identity is seen as a problem and not a solution.

Nevertheless, Transpersonal systems still leave something to be desired.

---

[18] Retrieved online at
http://www.adherents.com/Religions_By_Adherents.html

THE DIVIDE BETWEEN
EASTERN & WESTERN RELIGION

East and West create two radically different types of identities:

❖ Eastern-Transpersonal Identity: The World and Self are an Illusion. Nevertheless, you are obligated to do good, apropos of nothing.

❖ Western-Personal Identity: You are a Sinner in need of God's salvation. You must obey God's Word in order to be saved.

These two different views of identity can be conceived of as the two religious pillars that form the **Temple of Religious Consciousness**. The temple drawing illustrates the false dichotomy created when Personal and Transpersonal Divinities divided human Consciousness.

The Central Problem of the religions in the East and the West is that they divide human existence.

In its present form, the Temple of Religious Consciousness presents us with yet another arbitrary either/or in which the spiritual seeker can only select one of two basic identities.

In either case, one must be converted and conform to a given religious identity and set of practices.

I know from decades of intense spiritual practice – and "trial and error" is a better term for what went on in my own search for truth – that any form of religious identity can become an anchor around your neck. I created Day Teaching in order to transcend the problems inherent in conventional East/West practices.

RELIGIOUS CONVERSION

Religious "conversion" is exactly what it says it is: The conversion of Free Consciousness into a binding identity. A "bound identity" is an identity that has been locked into place by the great force of a person's own belief, need, and fear.

A bound identity cannot be easily unbound and, in fact, resists any attempt to unbind it from that to which it is bound.

Religious conversion is typically considered in terms of a person embracing a set of religious beliefs. However, this view does not fully appreciate the power and reality of religious conversion.

Day Teaching restates "religious belief" in more profound terms. We understand that the Divinities have the power to convert human Consciousness into Religious Identity.

Thus, religious conversion is an ***Identity-Creating and Locking Process***. This is a powerful mechanism insofar as a believer cooperates with the process whereby a Divinity converts their Consciousness into a religious identity – and this includes locking into place all of the hypocrisy and blindness inherent in any religious identity.

People enter into a relationship and communion with a Divinity for many reasons. However, the main reasons are to lead a better life, obtain forgiveness for one's sins, and to be assured of Heaven in the Afterlife.

Four of life's central questions are also immediately answered when a person surrenders their life to a Communion Divinity:

❖ Who am I?

❖ Where did I come from?

❖ What is the purpose of my life?

❖ What happens to me after I die?

As stated previously, religions that offer easy answers are very attractive to Souls who do not want to dig deep into their own Primal Matter to discover their true nature.

Having said that, the human Soul is ultimately of no real use to any Divinity whose stated purpose is to assimilate as many human Souls as possible.

To "Become One with God" actually means what it says: You will disappear into a Divinity and have no individuality for all of Eternity.

Is that what you really want?

Do you want to be someone else other than yourself?

DIVINE IDENTITY

When a human believes they are in "One" with the Creator-God of the Universe, then that person will not easily unconvert.

That person believes their eternal salvation depends upon maintaining their religious identity.

Secular people do not understand the profundity of religious conversion.

When a person's religious "beliefs" are challenged, ridiculed, or attacked, what is actually challenged or attacked is their core identity – which identity forms their sense of Reality.

Religious people can and do fight savagely to protect their core identity and sense of Reality.

Even when a person's identity and sense of Reality is based upon beliefs such as the Rapture or nonscientific stories such as Noah and the Ark, that person will nevertheless ruthlessly fight for their God, identity, and sense of Reality.

Religious people are easy to radicalize when they are attacked. Religious leaders know this and use it create a cultic "Us against Them" mentality for cynical, self-serving purposes ranging from fundraising, to a political agenda, to engaging in violence and war.

In the bigger picture, the mechanism of converting Consciousness to Identity occurs in all areas of human life.

Religion, politics, cults, multilevel marketing groups, special interest groups, and other groups that need money and labor are eager to give people a ready-made "plug and play identity" that fulfills the innate human need for meaning and purpose.

These groups also tend to radicalize their members and whip them into a frenzy so that they will wage propaganda wars, or even actual wars, against real and perceived enemies.

KEEPING RELIGIOUS IDENTITY LOCKED IN PLACE

"God" instantly becomes real when a person is saved inasmuch as there is a conversion from one's existing identity to a new and higher "energy state" of identity. In this case, the person has been energized, or seemingly made alive, by a Divinity. There is real spiritual transformation of the Soul. This is being born again.

Yet Salvation is not a stable energy state. The higher energy state is not guaranteed and typically fades. This fading is very common.

The believer can "backslide" and convert back to his or her old identity if one does not follow the Biblical admonitions to, among other things, do the following:

❖ Read and study the Word of God each and every day

❖ Crucify the Flesh daily

❖ Offer unceasing worship and prayers to God

All Communion Divinities demand that their converted followers read and memorize Scriptures and pray on a daily basis. This is why Communion Divinities demand that their followers formally gather together in temples, mosques, or churches several times a week – or even on a daily basis. Any disbelief or heresy is punished in ways ranging from excommunication to execution. The core identity must never be questioned or threatened.

SERVANT

If you honestly seek to communicate with a Divinity, you can indeed experience direct Divine psychoactive contact.

You do so at your own risk.

Baptism is an example of an initiatory activation of a Divinity within a human. Once a Divinity gets inside of you and begins to unfold, there will be an inner fight for control. Your God wants control of your Soul and yet you feel that it is your Soul to do with as you please.

The Divinities have never lied about this basic fact of religion: They want to assimilate human Souls into themselves.

Indeed, a reciprocal exchange of energy occurs in any Divinity-Worshiper covenant:

❖ A Divinity needs the energy of human worship to sustain their Divine identity. This is obviously true because the YHWH, Allah, and all other Divinities demand worship.

❖ Worshipers need the Divine Energy to sustain their religious identity. This is obviously true because worshipers worship daily. Any worshipper who fails to offer up daily worship is not worth their salt.

The Divinities who feed on human energy are called ***Communion Divinities***.

The term is used because the energy flow between Divine and human happens in communion. We do not use the word "communion" in the limited Christian sense of the sacrament of taking the body and blood of Christ. Rather, we use "communion" to mean the deep, abiding, and often demanding relationship between a Divinity and humans.

A Divinity makes extraordinary demands upon a human. "Sin" in this sense is the refusal of the believer to be converted into the image and likeness of their Divinity.

Sin is to miss the singular goal of conversion, which goal is to be assimilated into the Divinity. Moreover, Divine purposes are not always rational, or even logical, to the secular human mind.

The Divinities are not accountable to humans, human thinking, or the human demand for rationality or proof.

Divinities want to assimilate humans.

Therefore, take the Divinities at their word: You must become a servant and ultimately be assimilated into your God if you truly want to be One with him.

HIGHER STATES

Communion with a Divinity is not about Ascent into higher states of Consciousness. Higher states are forbidden by Communion Divinities in any case. That is why books like the Bible outlaw esoteric practices that open the powerful psychic energy centers in the human body. Conventional Religion is concerned with making people the servants of a Divinity and ultimately consuming their lives, money, and labors to serve Divine purposes.

Once a Communion Divinity is active inside of a person, it will begin the progressive work of bending that person to its Will.

A true psychoactive or spiritual relationship with a Communion Divinity requires a person to surrender and become absorbed into the Divine over time.

A human spiritual teacher is needed to instruct and supervise a student in such a relationship. These teachers are typically ordained and authorized by an organization. Hence, any organized religion arises as a function of protecting and perpetuating the identity and purposes of the Divinity it serves as well as its human leaders.

When in contact with humans, the Communion Divinities reduce their power so that they do not obliterate the human Soul.

As a general statement, the Divinities begin working with people by using beliefs and emotional effects within the Soul. Over time, as a believer surrenders their identity, they begin to experience increasing levels of Divine power in the Soul.

There is a ratio of ego to spiritual ability. The more egoic one is, the less they are allowed to see their Divinity or taste Divine Power. Only servants are trusted with genuine Divine power on the level of the Soul.

This is a frightening prospect to the extent that a religious leader with true power can order a holy war, executions, or even a Culture War that acts to polarize a society or nation over the issue of religion.

The Divinities can and do use their human servants to wreak havoc for one simple reason: Both the Divinity and his servants want to rule the World and establish a religious Theocracy. This is the essence of monotheism: The establishment of a global religious Theocracy by appeal, violence, or whatever else it takes.

THE URGE TOWARD INFINITY

To become "One with God" is the entire purpose of conventional religious systems.

The Communion Divinities embody the Urge toward Infinity.

The Urge toward Infinity is the desire to return to Infinity and live in our native state as Unified Consciousness.

The Communion Divinities offer an apparency, or imitation, of Infinity. Very often this imitation Infinity is driven by the strong, rapturous, and ecstatic feelings generated in an electronic worship service.

The electronic worship experience can become addictive inasmuch as it is rich in temporary catharsis and perhaps even endorphins generated by the hypno-electronic ecstasy of singing and worship. I know because I was once a Christian. I have impeccable credentials as a Jesus Person in the 1970's. Calvary Chapel Costa Mesa, etc. I discuss my spiritual path in detail in my next book.

At its best, communion with a Personal Divinity can approach the feeling of Infinity, of finding one's way back home. Yet, the trip always stops short, because Divinities are sub-Infinite.

Moreover, the Divinities have strict rules that require thought-stopping to prevent freethinking.

The Divinities have very strict rules that prohibit a true view of Infinity, as this would show them to be sub-Infinite and psycho-synthetic.

The Communion Divinities deflect their followers away from esoteric approaches to Infinity, preferring instead to lead Souls into the various Domains of Divine Psychoactivity.

For example:

- ❖ Christianity will put you into contact with The Elohim and their Proprietary Domain of Divine Psychoactivity.

- ❖ Islam will put you into contact with Allah and his Proprietary Domain of Divine Psychoactivity.

- ❖ Hinduism will connect you to its Divinities and their Proprietary Domains of Divine Psychoactivity.

Any religion worth its salt will be able to network you into its Divinity – providing that you meet the specified preconditions, some of which are cultic and arbitrary but nevertheless lead into a Proprietary Domain of Divine Psychoactivity.

Worshipping a Communion Divinity according to the dictates of one's own Conscience is a basic, inalienable human right.

All of us have the right to bind ourselves to a Divine Power.

All of us also have the inalienable right to reject the Divinities and their religions altogether.

We personally consider the Divinities to be enormous spiritual personalities who want to expand their respective **God Projects** at the expense of Humanity.

People become sheep when they allow a God or a ruler to dictate their identity. One of the historical vulnerabilities inherent in disunified Consciousness is that it does not know who it is.

Therefore, it will accept any number of identities thrust upon it by authority figures.

Day Teaching works to eliminate this vulnerability by informing people that they are disunified Consciousness arising prior to any identity. If any person can understand – even in principle – that they are Free Consciousness, then they do not need to be attached to an identity and endure all of the problems of identity.

Chapter Twenty-Three

RECONSIDERING CREATION STORIES ALTOGETHER

My work recasts religious Creation stories as ***Disunification Narratives***.

Creation Narratives are partial, imperfect descriptions of the Disunification as witnessed by various Divinities. These narratives were transmitted to human scribes and became the basis of religious scriptures.

Disunification Narratives are a cosmic version of the common problem of witnesses to an event seeing slightly different – or even entirely different – versions of the same event.

Creation Narratives conflict because they were transmitted by Divinities who saw and experienced the Disunification in many different ways and from differing points of view.

It is fascinating to look at Creation stories through the lens of Disunification.

For example, YHWH revealed his point of view to the unknown writers of the Pentateuch. One of the most famous religious passages in world history is Genesis 1:1:

"In the beginning God created the heavens and the earth."

Contrast Genesis 1:1 with Sura 21:32 of the Qur'an:

"Do the unbelievers not realize that the heaven and the earth used to be one solid mass that we exploded into existence? And from water we made all living things. Would they believe?"

Many contemporary Islamic commentaries claim that this verse confirms that the Qur'an correctly describes the Big Bang and biology. From our viewpoint, we see Sura 21:32 as Allah correctly describing both the Big Bang and water as the basis of biological life to Mohammed.

As Day Teaching views the matter, any Divinity would be **partially correct** in claiming Creator status in that they were part of the Dream Tribe.

YHWH used his Dream Tribe status to elevate himself to "Creator-God" on this side of the Disunification. Allah has made the same claim. We see them both as part of the Dream Tribe.

Creation mythologies abound because Divinities abound.

There were many Divinities who saw and experienced the Beginning. They indeed emerged from the Disunification as the uncreated authors of their own forms.

None of these Divinities were born. Like everyone else in this Universe, they preexisted in Infinity and were disunified. When they passed through Disunification, they were rendered sub-Infinite.

We therefore say that all religions contain some part of the **Infinite Gnosis**, or knowledge.

The doctrine of ***preexisting spirits*** is part of that knowledge. We therefore view religious creation stories as having two components:

- ❖ The first component consists of elements that happened prior to the Disunification. This is preexistent knowledge.

- ❖ The second component is what happened immediately after the Disunification. This is post-Disunification knowledge.

Both forms of knowledge were skewed by the Disunification and by the Divinities emerging into their respective identities.

Day Teaching offers a way to powerfully reconsider Creation stories altogether.

THE PRE-EXISTENCE OF EVERYBODY

Day Teaching is congruent with the ancient spiritual insight that we all preexisted as spirits prior to birth.

However, Day Teaching greatly extends this notion to say that the Divinities - and all other sentient beings in our Universe - pre-existed in Infinity before this Universe appeared.

By analogy to technology, we can say that we preexisted in Infinity as virtual people, i.e. as spirits. "Spirits" are redefined in my work as ***virtual people in Infinity*** awaiting embodiment in order to realize their personhood in our Universe - or any other physical universe .The doctrine of Pre-Existence occurs in:

- Judaism
- Greek Philosophy
- The work of Origen (185-254 A.D), an early Christian theologian
- Islam
- The Church of Jesus Christ of Latter Day Saints (Mormonism)

SCRIPTURE AS PREEXISTENT IMAGERY

Day Teaching maintains that we all pre-existed and were present at the Dreaming Pool.

On this basis, we conclude that those spiritual teachings which contain Preexistent Dreaming Pool Imagery have an extremely "high resonance and coupling energy" within the human psyche.

The major religions took root and grew, in part, because people feel natively attracted to the preexistent imagery and information religious scriptures offer.

Polytheism, Monotheism and all other forms of spirituality and religion are explained by Disunification.

The great moral and spiritual attraction to the Bible, the Qur'an, the Gitas, the Sutras, and many other religious scriptures are explained by the high density of preexistent imagery and information they contain.

JAINISM

Western science claims that the Big Bang was the beginning of everything. Western science wants to claim its discovery of the Big Bang in a sort of Jehovah way that allows them to brush off religion. Yet, prior to Edwin Hubble's discovery that space was expanding, Science believed that the Universe was static, had always existed, and never had a beginning.

Jainism, an ancient Indian religion that predates Buddhism, holds the same view. Writing at Jainworld.com, Dr. L. M. Singhvi states:

Jains do not acknowledge an intelligent first cause as the creator of the universe. The Jain theory is that the universe has no beginning or end. It is traced to jiva and ajiva, the two everlasting, uncreated, independent and coexisting categories. Consciousness is jiva. That which has no consciousness is ajiva. There are five substances of ajiva:

- *Dharma - the medium of motion*

- *Adharma - the medium of rest*

- *Akasha - space*

- *Pudgala - matter*

- *Kala - time*

Pudgala (matter) has form and consists of individual atoms (paramanu) and conglomerates of atoms (skandha) which can be seen, heard, smelt, tasted and/or touched. According to Jains, energy, or the phenomena of sound, darkness, shade, heat, light and the like, is produced by conglomerates of atoms.

While formulating Day Teaching, I arrived at something akin to jiva and ajiva, although differentiated due to the Disunification, the Big Bang, and Spirit and Matter.

CREATION STORIES:

CHAOS, DARKNESS, AND WATER

Chaos, darkness, and water are recurrent features noted in creation stories. As written in Genesis1:1-2 (NASB):

In the beginning God created the heavens and the earth. The earth was formless and void, and darkness was over the surface of the deep, and the Spirit of God was moving over the surface of the waters.

The Elohim describe the heavens and the earth as being formless, void, and dark. We take this as a description of the early Universe. In the beginning, our Universe was indeed formless, existed in a void of expanding space, and was dark. In fact, matter was so dense that light could not escape from the early Universe.

After about 500,000 years, an event called "photon decoupling" occurred. In this event, matter expanded sufficiently to allow light to shine. The Elohim would have remembered when the light dawned in our Universe because they were there as the Protogenoi. Therefore, The Elohim correctly inform us in Genesis that it was dark at the beginning of our Universe.

Because they are not bound to human time as their frame of reference, 500,000 years seemed like a brief interval to The Elohim. And because they see themselves as the sole Creator-God Collective, The Elohim claimed credit for the appearance of light. As written in the Book of Genesis 1:3-5:

Then God said, 'Let there be light'; and there was light. God saw that the light was good; and God separated the light from the darkness. God called the light day, and the darkness He called night. And there was evening and there was morning, one day.

Day and Night only have meaning on planets that revolve around stars. Day and night have no meaning in outer space. Seen from a contemporary perspective, the passage only has meaning with respect to our Sun and Earth and not to the Universe as a whole.

The Elohim never had, and never will have, an understanding of Science. This is to be expected as they are Consciousness and reject Nature as being defiled, evil, and fallen.

The Elohim do not exist in Nature and so understandably would not grasp its mechanics.

This lack of understanding Nature is reflected in their scriptures and followers.

Judeo-Christianity is notoriously anti-scientific.

THE JAPANESE CREATION MYTH

The Japanese creation myth comes from ***Kojiki*** (Records of Ancient Matters), a book of ancient stories written in 712 A.D. by O No Yasumaro.

This creation narrative repeats a common theme in such stories.

The theme is that each land and its people have unique, protective Divinities.

These Divinities helped to create the land and work to help the people.

The following first section of the Kojiki relates the beginning of the Universe as having occurred with the birth of five Divinities.

PART I - THE BIRTH OF THE DEITIES
THE BEGINNING OF HEAVEN AND EARTH

The names of the deities that were born in the Plain of High Heaven when the Heaven and Earth began were the deity Master-of-the-August-Center-of-Heaven; next, the High-August-Producing-Wondrous deity; next, the Divine-Producing-Wondrous deity. These three deities were all deities born alone, and hid their persons.

The names of the deities that were born next from a thing that sprouted up like unto a reed-shoot when the earth, young and like unto floating oil, drifted about medusa-like, were the Pleasant-Reed-Shoot-Prince-Elder deity, next the Heavenly-Eternally-Standing deity.

These two deities were likewise born alone, and hid their persons.

The five deities in the above list are separate Heavenly deities.

THE SEVEN DIVINE GENERATIONS

The names of the deities that were born next were the Earthly-Eternally-Standing deity; next, the Luxuriant-Integrating-Master deity. These two deities were likewise deities born alone, and hid their persons.

The names of the deities that were born next were the deity Mud-Earth-Lord; next, his Younger sister the deity -Mud-Earth-Lady; next, the Germ-Integrating deity; next, his younger sister the Life-Integrating-Deity; next, the deity of Elder-of-the-Great-Place; next, his younger sister the deity Elder-Lady-of-the-Great-Place; next, the deity Perfect-Exterior; next, his younger sister the deity Oh-Awful-Lady; next, the deity Izanagi or the Male-Who-Invites; next, his younger sister Izanami or the deity the Female-Who-Invites.

From the Earthly-Eternally-Standing deity down to the deity the Female-Who-Invites in the previous list are what are termed the Seven Divine Generations.

THE ISLAND OF ONOGORO

Hereupon all the Heavenly deities commanded the two deities His Augustness the Male-Who-Invites and Her Augustness the Female-Who-Invites, ordering them to "make, consolidate, and give birth to this drifting land." Granting to them a heavenly jeweled spear, they thus deigned to charge them. So the two deities, standing upon the Floating Bridge of Heaven pushed down the jeweled spear and stirred with it, whereupon, when they had stirred the brine till it went curdle-curdle, and drew the spear up, the brine that dripped down from the end of the spear was piled up and became an island. This is the Island of Onogoro.

COURTSHIP OF THE DEITIES

THE MALE-WHO-INVITES AND THE FEMALE-WHO-INVITES

Having descended from Heaven on to this island, they saw to the erection of a heavenly august pillar, they saw to the erection of a hall of eight fathoms. Then Izanagi, the Male-Who-Invites, said to Izanami, the Female-Who-Invites, "We should create children…

HUNGARY

The Hungarian creation story is contained in a book entitled, ***The Saga of the Legend of the Stag.***

In this narrative, humans were created from small seeds, or eyes, stored under the ocean.

These sorts of elements in creation myths have caused certain writers to speculate that humans were genetically engineered by ancient astronauts from other planets.

The Saga of the Legend of the Stag opens by mentioning the seeds of the Holy Sea:

The seeds of the Holy Sea break out of your shell.

The eternal sea's waves are waving, and rolling.

Their waves are rocking and their foam is hissing.
There is no earth yet anywhere, but in the immeasurable heights,
Above in his golden house, sits the great heavenly father on his golden throne.

He is the old, white haired and white bearded God of eternity.

On his black robes there are thousands of sparkling stars.
Besides him sits his wife, the Great Heavenly Mother.
On her white robes (palast) there are thousands of sparkling stars.

She is the ancient material of which everything is made.
They have existed from eternity in the past and will exist for all eternity to come.

In front of them stands their beautiful golden sunbeam haired son,
The sun God Magyar. The boy asks of his father:
"When shall we create the world of the humans my dear father?"

The Eternal Sea just waves and rolls.
Its waves are rocking and its foam is hissing.
The old gray-haired heavenly father lowers his head.
He ponders the question a while and a little longer,
Then he lifts his white haired head and talks to his son.

My dear sweet golden haired son, let us create then
For the humans their own world, so that they, who will be
Your children shall have a place to live in.

How shall we create such a world, my dear father?

This is the manner in which we can create it:
In the depths of the waving, blue Sea of Eternity are the
Sleeping eyes (seeds), sleeping seeds
The sleeping Magya's.

Descend therefore to the depths of the Great Sea.
Bring up the sleeping seeds and dreaming eyes, so that
We can create a world out of them…

From the surface of the sea bed, he brought up the
Sleeping eyes/ seeds, silver white small eyes.
The sleeping eyes awoke, the sleepy eyes opened and grew up and
became living beings.

THE NORDIC CREATION SAGA

Myths of the Norsemen: From the Eddas and Sagas, is a book on Norse mythology. Published in 1909, the book opens with the writer offering an overview of the Norse creation story:

When questioned concerning the creation of the world, the Northern scalds, or poets, whose songs are preserved in the Eddas and Sagas, declared that in the beginning, when there was as yet no earth, nor sea, nor air, when darkness rested over all, there existed a powerful being called Allfather, whom they dimly conceived as uncreated as well as unseen, and that whatever he willed came to pass.

In the centre of space there was, in the morning of time, a great abyss called Ginnunga-gap, the cleft of clefts, the yawning gulf, whose depths no eye could fathom, as it was enveloped in perpetual twilight. North of this abode was a space or world known as Nifl-heim, the home of mist and darkness, in the centre of which bubbled the exhaustless spring Hvergelmir, the seething cauldron, whose waters supplied twelve great streams known as the Elivagar. As the water of these streams flowed swiftly away from its source and encountered the cold blasts from the yawning gulf, it soon hardened into huge blocks of ice, which rolled downward into the immeasurable depths of the great abyss with a continual roar like thunder.

South of this dark chasm, and directly opposite Nifl-heim, the realm of mist, was another world called Muspells-heim, the home of elemental fire, where all was warmth and brightness, and whose frontiers were continually guarded by Surtur, the flame giant. This giant fiercely brandished his flashing sword, and continually sent forth great showers of sparks, which fell with a hissing sound upon the ice-blocks in the bottom of the abyss, and partly melted them by their heat.

Great Surtur, with his burning sword, Southward at Muspel's gate kept ward, And flashes of celestial flame, Life-giving, from the fire-world came."

The giant Surtur from Norse Mythology offers a fascinating contrast to Genesis.

In Genesis, YHWH stationed an angel with a flashing sword at the entry to Eden, to prevent Adam and Eve from re-entering the Garden.

In the Norse account, Surtur – a giant with a flashing, fiery sword – helps to melt the Abyss.

In terms of preexistence, this myth of the Nordic Divinities transmits quite a different perspective than that of The Elohim.

The giant Surtur and his flashing sword

Chapter Twenty-Four

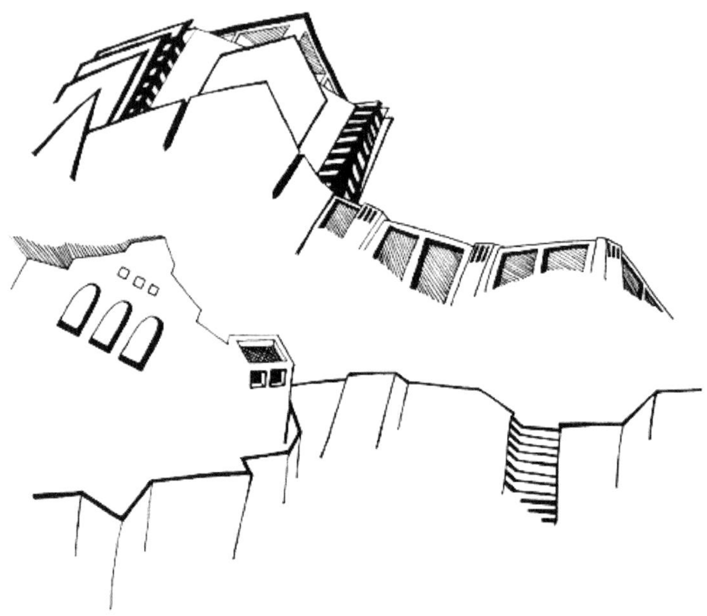

Temples Unfolding from Infinity, Cryptic Triptych, Panel Left
J. Augustine

THE BUDDHA

I bow out of deep respect to the Buddha.

His work has blessed me and taught me. During the hardest times of my life, I have retreated into my Buddhist Sanctuary located in the Palace of Nothingness. Of course, I decorate the ceiling of my Palace with Zen dragons, Hindu Goddesses, Christian Saints, and Masonic symbols as befits my need to be surrounded by Divinities and secrets hidden in plain sight. These deities may be either literal or metaphorical.

You decide.

Buddhism is a complex subject briefly touched in this chapter. There are many excellent books and retreats available for those who would like to begin their own investigation into Buddhism.

Buddhism is about attaining the single, powerful realization of the Buddha Nature.

Day Teaching considers the Buddha Nature to be a Transpersonal Divine Energy that is freely available to all beings.

The Buddha offered very specific and practical advice on how Buddhists are to put his teachings into practice. The Buddha first offered **The Four Noble Truths**:

- ❖ There is suffering (Dukkha)

- ❖ There is a cause of suffering (Craving)

- ❖ There is the cessation of suffering (Nirvana)

- ❖ There is the Eightfold Path leading to the Cessation of Suffering

The Buddha then articulated the ***Eightfold Path*** that leads to the cessation of suffering:

- ❖ Right Understanding

- ❖ Right Thought

- ❖ Right Speech

- ❖ Right Action

- ❖ Right Livelihood

- ❖ Right Effort

- ❖ Right Mindfulness

- ❖ Right Concentration

How does practice of the Eightfold Path translate in actual living?

Atisha, the 11th century Buddhist Master, listed thirteen qualities he considered the greatest expressions of Buddhist practice:

1. The greatest achievement is selflessness.

2. The greatest worth is self-mastery.

3. The greatest quality is seeking to serve others.

4. The greatest precept is continual awareness.

5. The greatest medicine is the emptiness of everything.

6. The greatest action is not conforming with the world's ways.

7. The greatest magic is transmuting the passions.

8. The greatest generosity is non-attachment.

9. The greatest goodness is a peaceful mind.

10. The greatest patience is humility.

11. The greatest effort is not concerned with results.

12. The greatest meditation is a mind that lets go.

13. The greatest wisdom is seeing through appearances.

The Buddha characterized Life as suffering. This suffering is caused by craving. If craving ends then suffering ends and Nirvana is attained.

To understand how ***craving*** is defined in Buddhism, you need to engage in a study of the subject.

Craving is not one thing in Buddhism. It is not as simple as craving food, sex, money, a new car, or a relationship. Craving is an active process, a series of links in a chain. Craving is described in a Buddhist Teaching called ***The Twelve Links of Dependent Origination.***[19]

---

[19] http://www.arrowriver.ca/dhamma/deporig.html

Buddhism is the intense and continuous observation of the mechanistic automaticities that arise within Consciousness – and in particular the illusory nature of identity and the very notion of "I."

Formal meditation allows a student to observe and pass through the various states of Consciousness and Spiritual Phenomena described in Buddhism.

THE COMPASSION OF THE BUDDHA

After his Enlightenment, the Buddha debated whether or not he should offer his teaching. An event described in the ***Ayacana Sutta: The Request***[20] from the Pali Canon describes how Buddha struggled with the elemental forces before vowing to teach the Dhamma:

THE Blessed One having attained Buddhahood while resting under the shepherd's Nigrodha tree on the banks of the river Neranjara, pronounced this solemn utterance:

How sure his pathway in this wood,
Who follows truth's unchanging call!
How blessed, to be kind and good,
And practice self-restraint in all!
How light, from passion to be free,
And sensual joys to let go by!
And yet his greatest bliss will be
When he has quelled the pride of 'I'.

I have recognized the deepest truth, which is sublime and peace-giving' but difficult to understand; for most men move in a sphere of worldly interests and find their delight in worldly desires. The worldling will not understand the doctrine, for to him there is happiness in selfhood only, and the bliss that lies in a complete surrender to truth is unintelligible to him. He will call resignation what to the enlightened mind is the purest joy. He will see annihilation where the perfected one finds immortality. He will regard as death what the conqueror of self knows to be life everlasting. The truth remains hidden from him who is in the bondage of hate and desire. Nirvana remains incomprehensible and mysterious to the vulgar whose minds are beclouded with worldly interests. Should I preach the doctrine and mankind not comprehend it, it would bring me only fatigue and trouble.

---

[20] Carus, Paul. Buddha, The Gospel, The Open Court Publishing Company, Chicago, 1894.

Mara, the Evil One, on hearing the words of the Blessed Buddha, approached and said: 'Be greeted, thou Holy One. Thou hast attained the highest bliss and it is time for thee to enter into the final Nirvana.'

Then Brahma Sahampati descended from the heavens and, having worshiped the Blessed One, said: 'Alas! the world must perish, should the Holy One, the Tathagata, decide not to teach the Dharma. Be merciful to those that struggle; have compassion upon the sufferers; pity the creatures who are hopelessly entangled in the snares of sorrow. There are some beings that are almost free from the dust of worldliness. If they hear not the doctrine preached, they will be lost. But if they hear it, they will believe and be saved.'

The Blessed One, full of compassion, looked with the eye of a Buddha upon all sentient creatures, and he saw among them beings whose minds were but scarcely covered by the dust of worldliness, who were of good disposition and easy to instruct. He saw some who were conscious of the dangers of lust and wrong doing. And the Blessed One said to Brahma Sahampati: 'Wide open be the door of immortality to all who have ears to hear. May they receive the Dharma with faith.'

"Then the Blessed One turned to Mara, saying: 'I shall not pass into the final Nirvana, O Evil One, until there be not only brethren and sisters of an Order, but also lay disciples of both sexes, who shall have become true hearers, wise, well trained, ready and learned, versed in the scriptures, fulfilling all the greater and lesser duties, correct in life, walking according to the precepts-until they, having thus themselves learned the doctrine, shall be able to give information to others concerning it, preach it, make it known, establish it, open it, minutely explain it, and make it clear-until they, when others start vain doctrines, shall be able to vanquish and refute them, and so to spread the wonderworking truth abroad. I shall not die until the pure religion of truth shall have become successful, prosperous, widespread, and popular in all its full extent-until, in a word, it shall have been well proclaimed among men!'

Then Brahma Sahampati understood that the Blessed One had granted his request and would preach the doctrine.

In so many ways, Disunified Life is suffering.

Perhaps it was because of Disunification that Brahma Sahampati came down from the Brahma-world and prevailed upon the Buddha One to teach the Dhamma

The Great Compassion of the Buddha is transpersonally present and active in our World.

The Buddha continues to teach through his words and followers. The Buddha was and remains one of the greatest World Teachers that ever lived.

"May all that have life be delivered from suffering."

– Gautama Buddha

Reeds

J. Augustine

PEELING THE ONION:

THE LAYERS AND AGGREGATES

It is possible to escape the Automated Embodiment Mechanics of the Disunification.

Buddhism offers one path and its tools are excellent.

How is transcendence accomplished in Buddhism?

How are the layers peeled away?

Buddha's teaching states that the egoic "I" consists of what he called the *five aggregates*:

- ❖ Form
- ❖ Feeling
- ❖ Conception
- ❖ Disposition
- ❖ Consciousness

Buddhism asserts that the five aggregates of which Consciousness is composed can be dismantled by the systematic practice of Buddhism.

The ultimate result of right practice is Nirvana, the cessation of suffering. The Buddha teaches that we can unweave the aggregates, so to speak, by use of his techniques.

For this reason, the Buddha is always working to break a student's mind.

Only by calling the student's *Process of Mind* constantly to attention and account can the Teacher keep breaking the Mind before it has a chance to dumb down the Teaching into beliefs.

Beliefs are not Enlightenment. The aggregates are therefore understood as a description and not something to believe.

TROUBLESHOOTING

The Buddha was, and remains, one of the world's best troubleshooters when it comes to human Consciousness. While Buddhists may protest that they are concerned only with Reality and not metaphysics, a surreptitious peek into their technical documentation reveals a treasure trove of jeweled boxes full of details about psycho-mechanics, angry ghosts, the body, FAQ's, and other tools for use in troubleshooting human existence.

A quick look at a Buddhist glossary shows the following entries just for the letter S. These entries all have to do with the Buddha, meditation, and the states and parts of Consciousness:

- samadhi
- samatha (Skt. shamatha)
- samsara
- samyojana
- Sangha
- sati (Skt. smrti, Jap. nen)
- Samadhi.
- Satipatthana Sutta
- sensei
- Shakyamuni
- Sage of the Shakya clan.
- Shingon
- Shinran Shonin
- skandha
- skillful means
- Siddhartha (Pali Siddhatta)
- Soka Gakkai International (SGI)
- soteriology
- sublime abidings
- sutra

Buddhism employs an extremely technical language, a knowledge of which allows a practitioner to trace down the constituent elements, moods, and sensations that arise within Consciousness.

Ultimately, the constituents are traceable to Nothingness.

This is a remarkable Realization: once you experience Nothingness your Consciousness is changed permanently. This happened to me and I learned to create from Nothing.

Buddhism liberates Consciousness from false beliefs and identities that are created by the Mind.

When you use Buddhism to begin the systematic processing of dismantling your Ego, you will quickly discover the illogical associative links that form your identity.

As you engage in Buddhist meditation over time, you become better able to distinguish Consciousness from Identity. You simultaneously acquire a Buddhist identity as this occurs.

Thus, your sense of Consciousness will become qualified and defined in terms of Buddhism.

To say "I am a Buddhist" is, after all, a statement of identity, meaning, and purpose. To be a Buddhist in the legalistic sense is as much of a trap as being a legalistic Christian or a Muslim.

FOURTEEN QUESTIONS THE BUDDHA WILL NOT ANSWER

Buddhism is noble, but it heavily discourages people from asking metaphysical questions deemed unrelated to their immediate life.

Indeed, the Buddha refused to answer fourteen specific questions.

These are called the ***Fourteen Unanswered Questions***:

- ❖ Questions referring to the world: concerning the existence of the world in time:
    - Is the world eternal?
    - or not?
    - or both?
    - or neither?

- ❖ Questions referring to the world: concerning the existence of the world in space:
    - Is the world finite?
    - or not?
    - or both?
    - or neither?

- ❖ Questions referring to personal experience:
    - Is the self identical with the body?
    - or is it different from the body?

- ❖ Questions referring to life after death:
    - Does the Buddha exist after death?
    - or not?
    - or both?
    - or neither?

Because Day Teaching understands humans as being both Personal and Transpersonal, there is no refusal to ask, explore, examine, or speculate upon any questions.

Because we are Disunified Awareness, we are free to explore all of the multiple dimensions of the human experience.

We can have a conversation about extraterrestrials as easily as we can discuss physics. These two discussions would of course be weighted in such a way as a as to grant physics gravity while remaining skeptical of the claims of Ufology. However, nothing is off limits to discussion inasmuch as we are ultimately dealing with Consciousness arising in an incredibly large Universe.

Although the Buddha did not approve of it, speculation is neither deadly nor forbidden. Speculation costs nothing, allows the mind to wander, and is one way to think outside the box.

Day Teaching encourages people to explore all models of reality in order to find answers.

When we explore the existing maps of Consciousness by use of Day Teaching, we add a dimension of understanding that has not previously been available.

YOU ARE NOT YOUR IDENTITY

When you realize that you are not obligated to your identity and its mechanistic moods, feelings, and thoughts then you simply allow them to arise and watch them.

They no longer control you as they once did because there is no "I" having Moods, Feelings, and Thoughts. There is fundamentally only disunified Awareness observing and experiencing the various motions and energies in the Body-Mind system.

As a consequence, perhaps even a paradox, you have far more free will and determination to do whatever you want when you come from a position of Consciousness. There is no internal identity for you to defend or justify.

If someone calls you a name, there is no "I" to defend.

There is a just a person out there saying things.

You can be compassionate and see that they are upset. Their anger and upset belongs to them and not to you. If you did something to upset them, you would of course naturally apologize, but you would not need to react to their anger or emotions in any way.

Non-reaction is developed over time and it is an extremely effective way to live life.

The tools of Buddhism can be used with great fluency to navigate and expand Consciousness and ultimately attain the Buddhist form of Enlightenment.

While my work is very informed by Buddhism, it is not Buddhism. I have a different mission, teaching and form of Enlightenment. Nevertheless, I acknowledge with deep gratitude that I have been beneficially instructed by the teaching of the Lord Buddha.

COMPARING BUDDHISM & MORMONISM

Nineteenth century America saw the founding of **The Church of Jesus Christ of Latter Day Saints**, a group more commonly known as the Mormons. In Mormonism, the goal is to become a God over one's own planet and kingdom.

Unlike Buddhists who want to break the cycle of birth and death, Mormons embrace the cycle because it allows them to become like their God and have their own planets, very large families, and control of their own destinies. From ***Teachings of the Prophet Joseph Smith***:

> *Here, then, is eternal life – to know the only wise and true God; and you have got to learn how to be Gods yourselves, and to be kings and priests to God, the same as all Gods have done before you,... To inherit the same power, the same glory and the same exaltation, until you arrive at the station of a God...*

Contrasting Buddhism with Mormonism reveals the polarities relative to Embodiment in Disunification.

Buddhists want to escape the cycle of birth and death while the Mormons want to perpetuate and exalt the cycle by having large families and many descendants in order to build their own Celestial Kingdoms.

This matter of reincarnation is something to think about:
- Do you want to reincarnate?
- Or not?
- Or both?
- Or neither?

Given that all possible histories exist in the Multiverse, you have been incarnated, reincarnated, not incarnated, and in a state of Oblivion at various times.

You will continue your trek across the Vast Spectrum of Consciousness in many forms until the end of time.

Day Teaching is intended to assist you on your trek.

Make my wisdom your wisdom, for I seek to unfold and expand you to Infinity.

ALL WORLDS HIGH & LOW

I have directly experienced Nirvana and the Higher Worlds. I have experienced all spiritual Worlds both high and low. There is nothing off limits to me or anyone else when one understands they are Consciousness on an unqualified basis. What exists in this realization is choice. I chose certain things and did not choose others. Therefore this book came into existence at the expense of other things. That is what I sovereignly chose.

I learned for myself and wrote that there is "desire without limitation/within this discipline of birth."

Nirvana can be attained, but once it is experienced, it is better to return here and help others. Working to free others from illusion and suffering is more meaningful than Permanent Nirvana. In any case, one no longer exists when they attain Nirvana. What stands out in Nirvana is compassion for others and so the desire to return arises. Hence, Nirvana is reversible. Were Nirvana irreversible there could be no choice and thus Consciousness could not exist in its present form.

To this point, the Wikipedia webpage discussing the Crazy Wisdom tradition in Tibetan Buddhism contains a remarkable comment and quotation:

"From a particular Buddhadharma spiritual lexicon and perspective, Georg Feuerstein implies nonduality in his equating the essence of Samsara and Nirvana as the root of crazy wisdom[21]:

> 'Crazy wisdom is the articulation in life of the realization that the phenomenal world (Sanskrit: samsara) and the transcendental Reality (Sanskrit: nirvana) share the same essence.[22]'"

Samsara and Nirvana do indeed share the same essence. Their common essence is Disunified Awareness. Neither is Infinite.

The crux of the matter is that one can choose to stand free of any phenomenal or transcendental identity once they understand and realize that all things arise within Disunification.

Therefore, one no longer seeks Nirvana while suffering Samsara. We just wouldn't do it that way in Day Teaching.

Both seeking and suffering begin to diminish and fade when one realizes and directly experiences that they are Consciousness prior to everything arising.

What emerges is a noticeably different quality in Consciousness in which one uses the liberating knowledge of Day Teaching to free themselves from all of the "junk code" of limiting beliefs, culture, religion, etc.

This junk code contains suffering and you don't need it.

---

[21] Comment and quotation retrieved from
http://en.wikipedia.org/wiki/Crazy_wisdom#cite_note-Feuerstein_1991_70-8

[22] FEUERSTEIN, GEORG (1991). "Holy Madness: The shock tactics and radical teachings of crazy-wise adepts, holy fools, and rascal gurus". *Yoga Journal* (New York: Paragon House). ISBN 1557782504.

Chapter Twenty-Five

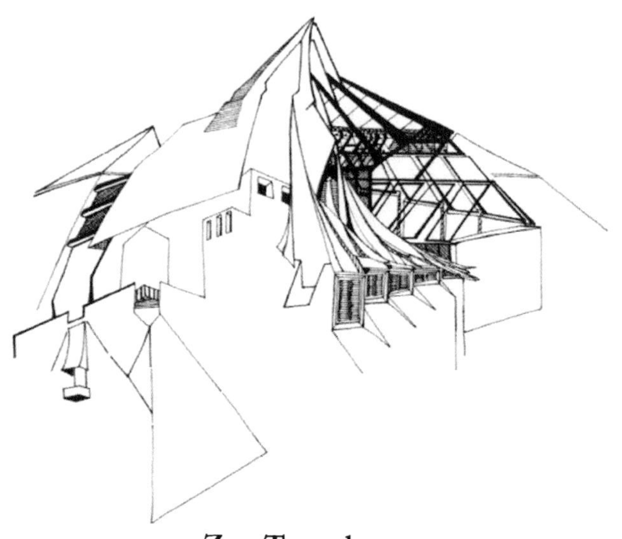

Zen Temple

J. Augustine

ZEN

What is the difference between Buddhism and Zen? Volumes have been written on this question and I cannot possibly do the topic justice in this present volume. Briefly, though, the basic question can be answered by way of Christianity. Christianity has two main denominations – Catholicism and Protestantism.

Each of these Denominations branches off into numerous smaller denominations, schools, sects, and independent churches

This same branching is true of Buddhism, for it also has two main schools: the **Mahayana** and **Theravada**.

The Buddha was born in India, thus making Buddhism Indian in origin. Buddhist monks carried his teaching to China where a distinctive Chinese form of Buddhism developed.

Bodhidharma is said to have been an Indian prince, a Buddhist, who traveled to China and originated Zen based upon Mahayana Buddhism. This happened sometime around the 7ᵗʰ century A.D. in China.

The Bodhidharma. Yoshitoshi (1839-1892), from an 1887 woodcut.

The Bodhidharma founded Zen based upon what he called, "a special transmission outside of scripture."

In other words, he found enlightenment outside of the written Buddhist scriptures.

This is akin to a Christian claiming a special revelation from God apart from the Bible. The Bodhidharma emphasized direct experience as opposed to blindly obeying the scriptures.

The Bodhidharma challenged Buddhist scholasticism. While Buddhist scholasticism is indeed impressive, it can also be ponderous and difficult.

The Bodhidharma said:

> ***Directly point to the human mind; see one's nature and become a Buddha; do not establish words and letters.***

Zen is based upon Buddhist DNA. However, Zen emphasizes looking directly at Life as opposed to formalizing experience in books of doctrine.

In Zen, one watches how the Mind chronically superimposes judgments and evaluations upon Life. The Mind is seen as an automaticity whose power can be broken by meditation and observation. Over time, the Eastern practitioner ceases to react to the Mind. "Do not react" is a mantra in both Zen and Buddhism.

Buddhism emphasizes scholasticism. It is imperative to learn Buddhist doctrine if one wishes to learn and practice Buddhism. However, an over-emphasis on doctrine can create legalistic distractions in meditation and daily practice.

Legalism deadens the practice of Buddhism or any other religion.

There are legalists in any religious or philosophical system that memorize "the book" and become experts in the book. They insist that all practice and life must follow the book. The slavish and mindless obedience to any Holy Book is indeed dangerous, especially when a Holy Book is used to radicalize people into violence.

Once religious zealots gain power, any behavior or thinking that is not "by the book" is punished. Jesus said that the letter kills but the Spirit gives life. By this, Jesus placed emphasis on experience and faith over obeying every "jot and tittle" of the Law.

Over time, Buddhism became increasingly formalized, scholastic, and hierarchical. This happens in any religion. This is why the Bodhidharma broke away. The work in Zen focuses on attaining a single, powerful, transforming realization: The Buddha Nature. Zen simply goes about it differently than Buddhism.

The so-called "Zen insight" is ineffable. Zen readily acknowledges the many problems caused by language: Enlightenment is made false by words. Yet, even Zen itself is infused by the language of SpiritMatter. No less an eminence than Thomas Merton had to invoke the language of SpiritMatter as he grappled to say what Zen is and is not. The bolded emphasis in the second paragraph of the quote below is mine:

> "The Zen insight cannot be communicated in any kind of doctrinal formula or even in a precise phenomenological description...And here of course we run into the first of

the abominable pitfalls that meet anyone who tries to write of Zen. For to suggest that it is 'an experience' which a 'subject' is capable of 'having' is to use terms that contradict all the implications of Zen.

"Hence it is quite false to imagine that Zen is sort of individualistic, subjective purity in which the mind seeks to rest and find spiritual refreshment by the discovery and enjoyment of his own interiority. It is not a subtle form of spiritual self-gratification, a repose in the depths of one's own inner silence. Nor is it by any means a simple withdrawal from the outer world of matter in an inner world of spirit. ***The first and most elementary fact about Zen is its abhorrence of this dualistic division between matter and spirit. Any criticism of Zen that presupposes such a division is, therefore, bound to go astray***[23]."

Zen abhors any duality. However, Zen must use the dualistic language of Spirit and Matter in order to have a duality which it can then abhor. This is an intrinsic problem with language and even Zen itself.

In any discussion of Consciousness, a duality is encountered – even if the duality is said to be illusory as it is in Zen.

Having identified SpiritMatter as the conceptual basis of Religion, we can see from the Thomas Merton quote above that Zen defines itself against SpiritMatter. The primacy of SpiritMatter is so great that both Buddhism and Zen must identify and protest duality in order to distinguish themselves as nondualistic systems.

---

[23] Merton, Thomas. Mystics & Zen Masters. Farrar, Straus and Giroux. 1999

"I"

Buddhism and Zen both look at all of the objects of body, mind, thought, and the Stream of Consciousness in such a way that there is no "I" looking.

In both disciplines, one coincides with existence and there is no "I" separating a person from Life. There is no "I" reacting to whatever arises. "I" is simply part of the arising experience itself. "I" is not granted separate ontological status in Zen.

A Zen practitioner does not identify him or herself with anything. Life is experienced directly. The judgments that the Ego, or the Mind, bring to Life are simply noticed. There is no attachment to sense of self and thus no need to defend a sense of self. There are no hurt or angry feelings to deal with when there is no "I" to have hurt or angry feelings. Instead, hurt and angry feelings arise, are observed like the weather, and are allowed to run their course and dissipate. "Do not react," is a key practice in Zen.

In Eastern schools, the physical world of the senses is deemed to be ultimately illusory. It is said to be **Maya**. A Sanskrit word meaning a **veil** or a **cover**, the word *Maya* is used to describe the persistent, inflexible illusion of the physical Universe to which we are bound.

The Eastern schools argue that what binds each of us to Maya is an unconscious Act of Identification. We identify ourselves with the illusion. We believe that we are our body, mind, thoughts, feelings, emotions, cravings, appetites, sexual desires, and so forth. We therefore act to defend our thoughts and feelings. We strive, fight, and even kill to fulfill our desires. We are in spiritual darkness, helplessly attached to our egoic dead-end lives, and cannot escape. This attachment to illusion causes great pain and suffering.

According to the Eastern schools, the trap we are in is called **Ego**. The Ego is a psychoactive process that can also be called **Mind**. Ego, Mind, and the System of Mind are synonymous. They are all Maya; they are all part of the Psycho-Synthetic Reality Process.

If one does not transcend the mechanics of the Mind, they are naturally bound to illusion by what seems like a great and unbreakable force.

The work in the Eastern disciplines of Buddhism and Zen is all about systematically deconstructing the illusion that one is the personal, fixed identity known as the Ego. This is done by methodically observing and transcending the mechanisms of identification and attachment via practice.

When one identifies completely with the Buddha Nature, all desires and attachments to things in the physical World are seen as detrimental to the enlightened, blissful state of Pure Consciousness. Bliss is ordinary: It is simple equanimity.

Desire and attachment create suffering. Therefore, the question asked is, "Who is the one suffering?" Upon investigation – at least according to Buddhism and Zen - there is actually no one found to be suffering. The sense of "I" is said to be an illusion.

Once the sense of "I" is transcended in a radical act of identification with Pure Consciousness, or God, suffering is no longer resisted by an egoic self. There is no "I" present to suffer.

Rather, Consciousness itself directly experienced and passes through suffering. Nothing is resisted; everything is directly experienced. We row our boats gently down the Stream of Life.

In Eastern work, one looks at the automated psychological structures in ego, mind, and feeling that cause upset and suffering. The work is to notice the chronic and involuntary nature of one's constantly chattering onboard psychological machinery.

By meditatively detaching from these mechanisms, by dis-identifying with them, suffering is lessened. The quality of one's life dramatically improves as excess baggage and false identifications are released.

There is always an internal voice judging and criticizing one's own self and others. Eastern spiritual work allows these critical thoughts to arise, be listened to without judgment, and then be released.

This method depowers the inner critical voice over time.

In fact, one learns that the inner critical voice is just a babbling machine that has nothing to do with you.

There is no need to identify with this blathering nonsense.

These are typical ego messages that repeat endlessly on a loop:

- ❖ Nothing is ever good enough.

- ❖ I am unhappy. I need someone or something else to be happy.

- ❖ Life today is bad. Life was better yesterday or will be better tomorrow.

Master Huang Po

On and on it goes. Buddhism and Zen offer powerful techniques that can be used to functionally detach one's consciousness from all of the chattering psycho-machinery.

The machinery is still there, but its force and volume are reduced as one expands their space and identifies more and more with Empty Consciousness, with the Buddha Nature.

Eastern metaphysics works to deconstruct the Ego and its automated mental chatter by using a potent technique of systematic observation.

This technique is simple. One begins by assuming they are nothing, that they are identical with the Void.

UNDERSTANDING

The Zen Master Huang Po wrote:

Men are afraid to forget their minds, fearing to fall through the Void with nothing to stay their fall. They do not know that the Void is not really void, but the realm of the real Dharma…

Once more, all phenomena are basically without existence, though you cannot now say that they are non-existent.

The substance of the Absolute is inwardly like wood or stone, in that it is motionless, and outwardly like the void, in that it is without bounds or obstructions. It is neither subjective nor objective, has no specific location, is formless, and cannot vanish.

The fundamental nature of all phenomena is close beside you, but you do not see even that; yet you still go on talking of your inability to see what is far away. What meaning can this sort of talk possibly have?[24]

Master Huang Po's insights are part of an incredibly important understanding.

When I overlay Day Teaching knowledge upon his description, I am able to see both the Self Non-Self aspect of the Disunification.

In a disunified Universe, all phenomena are basically without existence inasmuch as they are sub-Infinite, disunified constructs.

Yet, disunified phenomena are not now non-existent. Our Universe and Life are real and demonstrable.

The present moment – and all that is in it – is not now non-existent. Someday it will be non-existent, but it is not now. When you and I run out of Now, only then will we be non-existent.

---

[24] *The Zen Teaching of Huang Po* translated by John Blofeld

ZEN & DUST

Zen has likened irrational mental content to dust.

On this basis, Zen endeavors to solve the dust problem by either cleaning or removing the reflecting surface of Mind.

A famous Zen koan asks us:

If there is no mirror, where can the dust alight?

This line of enquiry led to a dust up, to a game of one-upmanship between two Zen Masters:

Gathas of Shen-hsiu and Hui-neng [25]
This body is the Bodhi-tree,
The soul is like a mirror bright;
Take heed to keep it always clean,
And let no dust collect on it. – **Shen-hsiu**

The Bodhi is not like the tree,
The mirror bright is nowhere shining;
As there is nothing from the first,
Where can the dust itself collect? – **Hui-neng**

Day Teaching does not seek to harmonize the disparate views of the venerable Masters Shen-hsiu and Hui-neng. We instead offer our own koan:

Consciousness is the tree,
Energy its mirror leaves;
When we look at Nature's trees
Mirror trees are the hardest to see.

---

[25] Gâthâs of Shen-hsiu (神秀 Jinshû) and Hui-neng (慧能 Enõ)
From Hui-neng's Platform Sûtra (T'an-ching 壇經/Dankyõ, full title Liu-tsu Ta-shih Fa-pao-t'an-ching 六祖大師法寶壇經 Rokuso Daishi Hõhõdankyõ)(Essays in Zen Buddhism – First Series 206, 207) Referenced from: Sacredtexts.com

Chapter Twenty-Six

The Data Forge in Infinity

J. Augustine

DISUNIFICATION & METAPHYSICS

This chapter contains some of my writings on the theme of Disunification Metaphysics.

The purpose is to show the approach I take to Metaphysics.

MOTION AND NECESSITY

The concept of the Universe as a series of nested concentric bodies, of enclosed spaces in a hierarchy, was conceived of in ancient times as shown in the drawing below.

This ancient depiction of the Cosmos evokes for me a sense of the Dirac Sea, a place where perpetual creation and annihilation occurs simultaneously.

An ancient concept of the Cosmos surrounded by an Infinite Atomic Chaos.

The Greeks devoted a great deal of thought to the nature, construction, and motions of the physical Universe. In the fifth century B.C. the Greek thinkers **Leucippus** and **Democritus** developed the theory that the Universe was based upon atoms and voids.

One can read about atoms and voids; motion and necessity; and of fragments at the Ancient Greek Philosophy website.

This superb website contains the following entry for Democritus of Abdera:

Atoms and Void

The theory of indivisible atoms should be regarded as a direct reply to Eleatic monism and in particular to Zeno's argument of infinite divisibility. Contra the Eleatic absolute denial of non-being, the Atomists state that non-being exists as emptiness: 'what-is' (to den) is the plenum of atoms, while 'what-is-not' (to meden) is the emptiness of void (kenon). Emptiness can explain natural phenomena and physical plurality; what-is-not is in existence spatially as the fundamental prerequisite of physical motion.

Motion and Necessity

Physical motion is the result of reason (logos) and necessity (anagke) and not of divine justice or moral law (dyke). Generation is an arbitrary motion from one state of atomic conglomeration to another through void. A structure of infinite uncuttable and invisible atoms lies behind the world of everyday experience, and consequently perceptible qualities are merely by convention. Reality consists only of atoms and void.

Fragments

[1] Leucippus of Elea or Miletus (both accounts are current) had associated with Parmenides in philosophy, but in his view of reality he did not follow the same path as Parmenides and Xenophanes but rather, it seems, the opposite path. For while they regarded the whole as one, motionless, uncreated, and limited, and forbade even the search for what is not, he posited innumerable elements in perpetual motion—namely the atoms—and held that the number of their shapes was infinite, on the ground that there was no reason why any atom should be of one shape rather than another; for he observed too that coming-into-being and change are incessant in the world. Further he held that not-being exists as well as being, and the two are equally the causes of things coming-into-being. The nature of atoms he supposed to be compact and full; that, he said, was being, and it moved in the void, which he called not-being and held to exist no less than being. In the same way his associate, Democritus of Abdera, posited as principles the full and the void.[26]

Day Teaching's distinction between Infinity and our Universe allows for a philosophical excursion into the nature of reality that conforms to ancient Greek notions. We can say of Disunification that, "Physical motion is the result of reason (*logos*) and necessity (*anagke*) and not of divine justice or moral law (*dyke*)." Disunification is the Logos and Anagke, the reason and necessity of Infinity.

---

[26] Retrieved online at: http://www.philosophy.gr/

In our Universe there is no absolute divine justice or moral law needed to compel or cause physical motion at the molecular and atomic levels.

Newtonian physics explains the laws and motions so well that scientists can park probes on Mars at exact XYZ Cartesian coordinates at a predetermined time and date. Sometimes, of course, we miss the Red Planet:

The Planet Mars.from the Hubble Space Telescope[27]

---

[27] Mars image retrieved online at:
http://www.nasa.gov/multimedia/imagegallery/image_feature_85.html

SAINT AUGUSTINE

The great Catholic theologian St. Augustine of Hippo (354-430) knew that motion was a necessary part of Creation, for nothing could exist without motion.

Augustine further argued that his God created the Universe **Ex Nihilo**, a Latin term meaning **from nothing**.

Some Christians take St. Augustine's work as evidence that he was describing the Big Bang.

St. Augustine addressed his doctrine of Creation Ex Nihilo in Book XI, Chapter VI of his legendary book **The City of God**.

CHAPTER VI - THAT THE WORLD AND TIME HAD BOTH ONE BEGINNING, AND THE ONE DID NOT ANTICIPATE THE OTHER.

For if eternity and time are rightly distinguished by this, that time does not exist without some movement and transition, while in eternity there is no change, who does not see that there could have been no time had not some creature been made, which by some motion could give birth to change — the various parts of which motion and change, as they cannot be simultaneous, succeed one another — and thus, in these shorter or longer intervals of duration, time would begin?

Since then, God, in whose eternity is no change at all, is the Creator and Ordainer of time, I do not see how He can be said to have created the world after spaces of time had elapsed, unless it be said that prior to the world there was some creature by whose movement time could pass.

And if the sacred and infallible Scriptures say that in the beginning God created the heavens and the earth, in order that it may be understood that He had made nothing previously — for if He had made anything before the rest, this thing would rather be said to have been made 'in the beginning,' — then assuredly the world was made, not in time, but simultaneously with time....

St. Augustine argues that the phrase "In the beginning" in Genesis 1:1 means exactly that: ***Nothing*** existed prior to our Universe.

St. Augustine reasoned that if God had created anything – whether it was time, place, or creature – prior to our Universe, then that would have constituted a prior beginning.

St. Augustine thus concludes that when Genesis 1:1 says, "In the ***beginning*** God created…" this was the <u>only</u> beginning.

There could not have ever been any other beginning or God would have stated such in the Scripture.

God had to have created us from nothing, Augustine reasons, for nothing is all that could have logically existed prior to the Biblical creation.

Day Teaching counters St. Augustine with its conception that LELA disunified the Universe from something – namely the preexistent Primal Matter – but that Disunification took place inside of the finite Nothingness of our Universe.

In the beginning, then, there was both something and nothing.

THE DIFFERENCE BETWEEN INFINITY & ETERNITY

We have already defined Eternity as the finite lifetime of a universe. St. Augustine, on the other hand, defined Eternity as the place in which God lives when he speaks of "God's eternity."

St. Augustine had an intellectual need to locate God somewhere and so he located God in Eternity.

Yet, if God dwells in Eternity, then Eternity would be greater than God insofar as Eternity could contain God.

Thus, the idea of God "dwelling in eternity" would certainly appear to violate the premise that nothing can be greater than God.

While the Infinite God does not dwell in our Universe, many powerful sub-Infinite Divinities do exist here.

THE KABBALAH

The concept of the "Ein Sof" is central to the Kabbalah:

Ein Sof (sometimes transliterated as Ayn Sof) refers to the infinite Divine (or G-d). In Hebrew Ein Sof means "Boundlessness," but is usually translated as "Without End." Often it is referred to as the "Infinite No-Thingness." It should be understood that this does NOT mean that Ein Sof is "nothing" for It is NOT a THING, but is a "somethingness" that we cannot define in human terms. Ein Sof, in the Kabbalistic tradition, is the ultimate source of all creation or existence.[28]

Isaac Luria (1534-1572) – the greatest of all Kabbalistic teachers – described the Ein Sof, or God, contracting down in order to create the universe:

Prior to Creation, there was only the infinite Or Ein Sof filling all existence. When it arose in G-d's Will to create worlds and emanate the emanated...

...He contracted (in Hebrew "tzimtzum") Himself in the point at the center, in the very center of His light. He restricted that light, distancing it to the sides surrounding the central point, so that there remained a void, a hollow empty space, away from the central point... After this tzimtzum... He drew down from the Or Ein Sof a single straight line [of light] from His light surrounding [the void] from above to below [into the void], and it chained down descending into that void.... In the space of that void He emanated, created, formed and made all the worlds.[29]

What contracts in Day Teaching is the Black Pearl, which we conceived of as a wave function or a virtual object in Infinity. This virtual object was not God or Infinity contracting "himself" down as proposed in the Kabbalah.

---

[28] Retrieved online at: http://www.einsof.org/
[29] Etz Chaim, Arizal *Heichal*, A"K, anaf 2

HERMETIC PHILOSOPHY

Hermetic philosophy traces its origins to the ancient and venerable Hermes Trismegistus.

The Kybalion: Hermetic Philosophy was published in 1908 by three unknown authors who called themselves "the Three Initiates."

The book summarized the seven central principles of Hermetic philosophy which are quoted below:

1. The Principle of Mind: The All is Mind, the Universe is Mental.

2. The Principle of Correspondence: As it is above, so it is below; as it is below, so it is above

3. The Principle of Vibration: Nothing rests; everything moves; everything vibrates.

4. The Principle of Polarity: Everything is dual, everything has poles; everything has its opposite: like and unlike are the same; opposites are identical in nature but different in degree; extremes meet; all truths are but half-truths; all paradoxes can be reconciled.

5. The Principle of Rhythm: Everything ebbs and flows, goes up and comes down; the pendulum swing is present in everything; the swing to the right is equal to the swing to the left; rhythm is the compensation.

6. The Principle of Cause and Effect: Every cause has an effect, every effect has a cause; everything happens according to the law. Chance is nothing more than the name that is given to an unknown law; there are many planes of causation, yet none escape this law."

7. The Principle of Gender: Gender is within everything; everything has its masculine and its feminine principles; gender manifests on all planes.

Day Teaching is not Hermetic. However, it appreciates the grand upward ascent and syncretism of Hermetic philosophy.

It is, after all, axiomatic in Day Teaching that everything must keep expanding, intertwining, recombining, and branching out into new forms.

Hermeticism is a tremendous expression of esoteric Renaissance spirituality, as are many other Mystery schools:

- ❖ Freemasonry
- ❖ Alchemy
- ❖ Kabbalah
- ❖ Rosicrucianism

These ancient teachings will always be with us in one form or another. Their work and influence are profound.

One of the most stunning symbols of Alchemy – or of any spiritual discipline – is the *Rose Cross*. This symbol is a 14th century Rosicrucian attempt to visually depict the various esoteric interactions of Spirit and Matter.

I am a Master Mason and a Knight Templar. However, this book and my work are not Masonic in nature.

DEISM

In the 17th century, Humanists riding on the wave of Science began to explicitly decouple their individual identity from the larger cultural Christian identity.

Not everyone wanted to be a Christian, and, many proto-Atheists became Deists as a way to step away from Christian identity while stopping short of openly rejecting a belief in God.

Deism is the belief that the vaguely-defined "watchmaker" Creator-God who designed and created the Universe and then left it alone to operate based upon known natural laws, or by natural laws that could be discovered by the human intellect.

Deism allowed secular-minded people to declare a belief in a distant, vaguely defined God and thereby remain safe from public censure, for it was not culturally acceptable to be an Atheist.

While the term Atheist was coined in the 16th century to describe godlessness, it is generally considered that people did not openly declare themselves to be Atheists until the 18th century.

PHYSICS AND THE RESURRECTION OF THE DEAD

Religion and Science have become bitter enemies over the origins of the Universe, genetic engineering, euthanasia, and other issues. And yet the lines between Religion and Science so easily blur on the edges when a scientist wants to argue morality or when a believer happens to be a physicist.

The eminent Christian physicist Dr. Frank J. Tipler, of Tulane University, has worked to establish the premise that God and Physics are not incompatible. In 1994, Tipler wrote a notable book entitled, ***The Physics of Immortality: Modern Cosmology, God and The Resurrection of the Dead.***[30]

In this book, Tipler presents his Omega Point hypothesis. Essentially, Tipler argues that we will all be resurrected from the dead when our Universe collapses down at the end of time. However, the resurrection Tipler describes will be a virtual event created inside of computers that have near-infinite computational power.

Powered by energy scavenged from the collapsing Universe, these astonishing computers will allow everyone that has ever lived to be resurrected and to live seemingly for eternity at the end of time. Tipler asserts that the Universe will end in a singularity that is God. Tippler also attempts to reclassify theology by asserting:

> "…that theology is a branch of physics, that physicists can infer by calculation the existence of the God and the likelihood of the resurrection of the dead to eternal life in exactly the same way as physicists calculate the properties of electrons. One naturally wonders if I am serious."

Dr. Tippler is indeed very serious or he would not have written his exceedingly ambitious book that infers the existence of God and the resurrection of the dead based upon physics.

---

[30] Tipler, Frank. The Physics of Immortality Modern Cosmology: God and the resurrection of the dead. Knopf Doubleday Publishing Group, London, 1997.

CONSILIENCE

The esteemed Harvard biologist Edward O. Wilson declared a pervasive view within Scientism in the pages of his noted work, **Consilience**, when he wrote:

> "We have come to the crucial stage in the history of biology when religion itself is subject to the explanations of the natural sciences… sociobiology can account for the very origin of the mythology by the principle of natural selection acting on the genetically evolving material structure of the human brain. If this interpretation is correct, the final decisive edge enjoyed by scientific naturalism will come from its capacity to explain traditional religion, its chief competitor, as a wholly material phenomenon. Theology is not likely to survive as an independent intellectual discipline. But religion itself will endure for a long time as a vital force in society…"[31]

The doctors Wilson and Tippler are both deeply involved in science and yet have derived vastly different conclusions about the ultimate nature of reality.

To rephrase the classic wisdom, good people will have honest disagreements about competing Models of Reality.

---

[31] Wilson, Edward O. Consilience: The unity of knowledge. New York: Knopf : Distributed by Random House, 1998.

IMMUTABILITY & CHANGE

One thing I have learned in my own private spiritual work is that certain things are unique and immutable to my own personhood.

On the other hand, I have annihilated much of my own Karma as if it were, "snow being thrown into a roaring furnace."

That which I found to be illusory disappeared, or, it became of no concern to me whatsoever.

I acknowledge that my own being includes the expanse of Good and Evil.

I acknowledge the Evil within me and seek to not empower or engage in it, this to the utmost of my power.

I do this as a matter of my own self-determined morality and as a function of taking full personal responsibility for my own life.

I alone am responsible for my own actions and so I seek to live a life that creates Good Karma. Where I have made mistakes I have paid dearly for my sins.

I seek to find the Truth.

As a consequence of my search for Truth, I found that no previous spiritual models were sufficient to satisfactorily explain Consciousness to me.

Therefore, I created Day Teaching in order to expand my own Consciousness and that of others who can hear what I am saying. I have always given myself the complete freedom to think about and explore whatever I want to think about and explore.

SECTION VI

CLOUD MECHANICS

Joshua Tree in the Mojave Desert

J. Augustine 2010

This final section concludes with an exploration of Disunification Metaphysics in terms of the Bardo and Cloud Mechanics.

Chapter Twenty-Seven

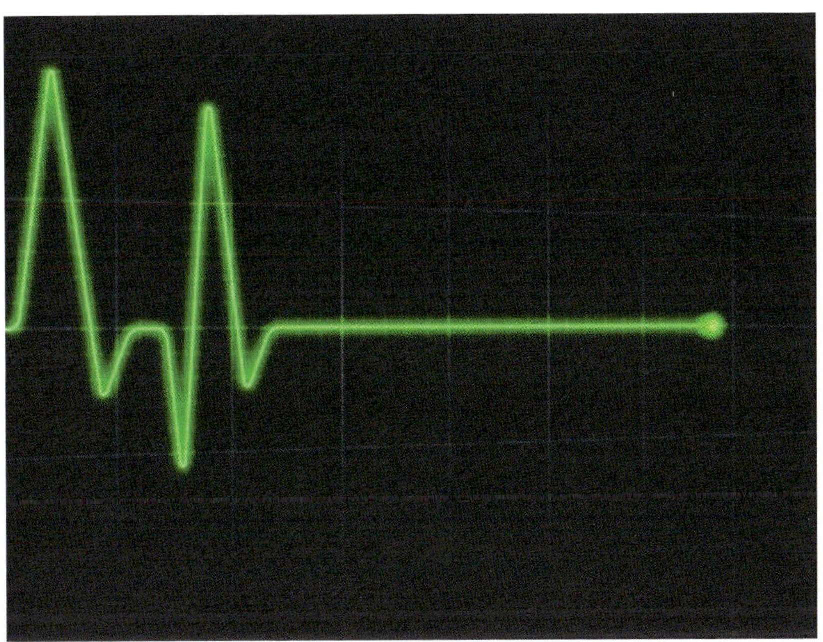

WHAT HAPPENS AFTER YOU DIE?

People want to know what happens after they die.

We offer our basic teaching on Death in this chapter.

If you have been a Good person, you need not fear Death or the Afterlife. You may experience fear or terror in your Death, but that quickly passes as you ascend into the Light.

If you have been Evil, the Afterlife will be brutal for you even as you were brutal. When you die, the Darkness will quickly enclose you as you descend into your self-created Nightmare.

If you are somewhere in between, Death and the Afterlife will be an intense experience in which you are placed on trial to determine the fate of your rebirth. It will be Purgatory. From the Latin, "Purgatory" means to cleanse or purge. Hence Purgatory is a place in which one is cleansed and purged.

Each and every death is unique because each of us has a part in generating our own Death and Afterlife experience. What the spiritual traditions say is true: The type of life you have lived and the state of your Consciousness at death directly affects your Afterlife. Consciously or unconsciously, you create a part of your own death experience.

This chapter uses some very classical concepts regarding the Afterlife. What we emphasize is that Death and the Afterlife occur within the Cloud of Life. The places we describe in this chapter are therefore "States of Consciousness" that have particular spiritual energy levels.

When you die, your Light Body is pulled into whatever region of the Afterlife matches your particular spiritual energy level. This is how Karma works in the Afterlife: You die and then flow along the path of least resistance. This is how you end up exactly where you belong. It is all "frequency-matching" so to speak.

At the moment of Death, your physical body releases its grip on your Light Body. This is where the "silver cord" is cut. The "silver cord" is the tether your Light Body uses to network and anchor itself into the physical body. This tether can be thought of as a complex set of data cables that runs through what has been called the chakras, or energy centers of the body.

As you are dying, the silver cord data cables begin to disconnect from the body. As this happens, the perceptual limitations – or what we can call the firewall of the physical body – are disconnected. This is when you suddenly begin to see and experience the "other side" and realize that your body has died.

The "other side" is that part of the Spectrum of Consciousness that is inaccessible due to the ***perceptual firewall*** imposed by the physical body. In the minutes, hours, and days following bodily death, most people can see their deceased body and the events surrounding their death while also seeing and experiencing the "other side."

While the Light Body is telepathic in nature, if you did not develop or use telepathy in life you will not have it after death. We define "telepathy" here as the natural sensitivity, or feeling, of knowing when someone is thinking about us. It is also the sense of knowing who is calling when the phone rings or knowing that you need to call or text someone.

There is nothing supernatural in telepathy.

We see it as a simple matter of being networked into the Cloud of Life.

When your body dies, your access to the Cloud expands and so any spiritual abilities you used in life greatly amplify as a result.

This is why some people who have died can "send messages" to their loved ones and others cannot.

LOSS

Central to Death is the complete loss of one's body and life. It all instantly ends at death. When you die you enter the region of Consciousness that exists between Birth and Death.

This region has been called by many names.

This chapter uses three words interchangeably, although they have different inflections and connotations in Day Teaching:

❖ The Afterlife: This term refers to the region of Consciousness we enter after the physical body dies.

❖ The White Light Tunnel: This refers to the state immediately after death. This state only lasts a few hours.

❖ The Bardo: The Tibetan Buddhist term Bardo is used to define the intermediate state between Birth and Death. Hence, Bardo has the specific connotation that one has died and has not yet been reborn.

While Day Teaching does not adhere to the strict meaning of the Buddhist technical term **Bardo**, we nevertheless employ the word as it conveys the sense of the profound Karmic processes that occur after death and determines rebirth.

The Bardo has no physical location because it occurs within Consciousness.

To get a sense of Bardo you can do this short exercise when seated in a chair and not distracted by anything:

❖ Imagine an incredibly vivid dream you had.

❖ Now imagine that you cannot wake up from this dream because:

> ➢ Your body has just died and you are now outside of the body.

> ➢ The White Light Tunnel experience of Bliss has come and gone.

> ➢ A dead loved one has appeared to tell you that you have died and crossed over to the other side.

> ➢ The crushing realization that you have died suddenly hits you. You realize that you are not going to be one of the lucky people who survive to talk about their Near Death Experience. Rather, you have now become someone who died.

The common denominator in Out of Body an experience is that people do not die nor do they lose their identity as a result.

A person's identity may shift or expand as a result of an Out of Body an experience, but identity itself is not lost.

Conversely, death fundamentally destroys the landscape of a person's identity.

Here are just some of the costs exacted by Death:

❖ The forfeiture of your body: This loss results in your instant bodily exclusion from the physical World.

❖ The loss of your name: Your body had a name and it died. You can look on your gravestone or watch your ashes be blown to the wind to confirm that who you were is now dead.

❖ Who are you when you no longer have a body and a name?

❖ The loss of your body, family, friends, and possessions – everything instantly gone.

❖ You have no voice, presence, or standing on the Earth. You are suddenly someone who has died.

YOUR LIFE FLASHING
BEFORE YOUR EYES

When you are dying, or come very close to dying, you might see your life flash before your eyes. This "flashing" is the Light Body performing a massive upload of your life into the Cloud of Life. This upload occurs whether you see it or not. In many cases, people are so understandably terrorized by their death that the last thing they notice is the upload.

This upload includes every detail of your life and is merged into all other uploads from our World and the Universe. A true and faithful record of our Universe is stored in that part of the Cloud that has been called the Cosmic Mandala.

The sum total of this archival activity will be uploaded into Infinity when our Universe ends.

My life flashed before my eyes once when I almost drowned at Huntington Beach here in Southern California. I was a child who ventured out too far. A large wave suddenly dragged me underwater and pinned me down with its great weight and speed.

As I tumbled wildly under the very edge of the Pacific Ocean, I could see the blue sky through the crystal clear green ocean water, frothing sea foam, and bubbles.

Despite struggling in terror to come up for air, I could not overcome the speed and weight of the wave in which I was trapped. I could no longer hold my breath and was starting to black out as my lungs burned from lack of oxygen.

My life flashed before my eyes when the realization hit me that I was going to drown so close to shore. Suddenly, I was thrust up above the wave and sucked in the biggest breath I had ever taken.

What struck me was that I had escaped drowning by a few seconds and that my very brief life had flashed before my eyes. Because I have native spiritual abilities and had lived and died countless times, I knew exactly what had just happened.

This made the event somehow less terrifying and I was grateful to have escaped Death.

THE WHITE LIGHT TUNNEL

Near Death Experiences are not of the same magnitude or nature as the total and irreversible death of the brain and body. What Near Death Experiences show us is a very good approximation of what actually happens in the first hours after death.

When your body dies, you continue on for a very short time with essentially the same sense of identity and level of self-awareness you have right now. If you have been a Good person and lead a Good life, you enter the legendary White Light Tunnel.

Like attracts Like. The White Light Tunnel is the spectacularly attractive luminous gateway into the Good Afterlife. As a Good Soul, you will be attracted to what is essentially your own nature.

Love and Bliss are pure essences and pull Good Souls into themselves. The White Light Tunnel is the gateway into the Elysian Fields, the place where those who were Good in the life go for refreshment and succor between lives.

Not all people who die see the White Light. Wicked Souls enter into a hellish Bardo that is intensely terrifying.

In the Bardo, those things we have done in our lives are reflected back to us in a powerful series of self-created and other-spirit-created hallucinations that are absolutely real and binding upon us.

There are other beings in the Bardo. These other beings have been classically described as angels or demons and that is basically what they are. As a part of the larger field of Consciousness, the Bardo is a Karma World that tries all Souls.

GHOSTS

Ghosts are a Bardo phenomenon. Specifically, ghosts are the Souls of the departed that exist in the boundary region of the Bardo that adjoins the human dimension. Ghosts have unfinished business that keeps them on the edge between this dimension and the Afterlife.

Some ghosts remain here for a few weeks as "short period dwellers" and can be called *shades*. Other souls become more intense and amplify into *ghosts* that haunt places. Ghosts are associated with:

➢ The need to communicate something left unsaid to a loved one

➢ Premature death, i.e. dying before one's time

➢ Sudden and violent death

➢ The need for Justice for their murder

Ghosts all have something going on or they would not stay and haunt the boundary region between Life and Death. Esoterically speaking, Ghosts are on the very periphery of the Tunnel of White Light.

They have not gone into the Tunnel.

What ghosts are doing is quite different from the gentle communications many of us have received from departed loved ones who are in the Bardo.

THE GARDEN OF EARTHLY DELIGHTS

Hieronymus Bosch's triptych entitled **The Garden of Earthly Delights** is of fascinating design and construction.

Made of three panels, the outer two panels close to form a painting of the tranquil Earth; this presumably as Earth existed before the Fall.

When the outer doors are opened, as shown below, a vast phantasmagorical panorama unfolds to the viewer:

Left Panel: Adam and Eve in the Garden
Center Panel: The Garden of Earthly Delights represented as a lusty
Right Panel: Hell, the place where all sinners reside eternally.

The Garden of Earthly Delights is Bosch's biblical-themed masterwork, for in it he links the Genesis story of Adam and Eve directly to Hell, via the wicked carnal excesses of life.

The essence of the biblical message is true: If you lead an evil life, you will pay for it in this life and in dire ways after you die.

While Day Teaching explicitly rejects as malicious the notion of ***eternal*** damnation as taught in Christianity, we recognize that the holy books offer descriptions of Heaven and Hell for a reason: The Afterlife and Karma exist as feedback systems in Consciousness.

What happens to a person in the Afterlife is the result of the deeds that person has done in life.

No one is punished in the Afterlife for what they believed or did not believe in life about God.

Having the "right beliefs" about God has nothing to do with the Afterlife because beliefs pertain only to identity.

"God" does not punish anyone in the Afterlife. The Bliss or Torment in the Bardo occurs purely as a function of one's own Karma.

The Bardo is a Karmic feedback system that exists within Consciousness:

➢ "Heaven" affirms one's evolutionary trajectory as a spiritual being.

➢ "Hell" rejects one's evolutionary trajectory as a spiritual being.

Bosch's triptych clearly shows the imprint of Catholic teachings upon him.

Artists in other religious traditions have produced different depictions of the Afterlife with the same themes of reward.

Hinduism calls Hell ***Naraka***.

The Hindu God of Death named *Yama* is seen seated in the center of his kingdom of death and judgment.

Seated to Yama's right is ***Chitragupta***, the Deity who records all human actions.

These actions are reviewed at death in order to determine one's Bardo and rebirth.

Karma is always something you do to yourself.

You will only realize this when you unknot yourself into the larger Spectrum of Consciousness.

An identity cannot see or even understand this fact.

The way in which Karmic Afterlife states manifest is unique to each person.

However, the common traits described in the classical spiritual literature are true: Heaven is an incredible Paradise. Hell is a terrible and anguished place of intense suffering.

TARTARUS & LIMBO

Tartarus is a spiritual term from ancient Greece that is not used anymore.

Day Teaching revives the term to describe the antithesis of the White Light Tunnel. Theoi.com says of Tartarus:

> "TARTAROS was the prison of the damned, a region in Haides where the souls of wicked men were condemned by the Judges of the Dead to a period of enforced purgatory, or, for the truly unredeemable, to eternal damnation.[32]"

Day Teaching agrees with the notion of Tartarus. There is a place of punishment and torment in the Afterlife. People are there because of what they did in life. The various names of Heaven, Hell, and Purgatory are unimportant. What is important is the truth: You reap what you sew.

In the remarkable Encyclopedia Mythica, Martha Thompson writes of Tartarus:

> "Tartarus is the lowest region of the world, as far below earth as earth is from heaven. According to the Greek poet Hesiod, a bronze anvil falling from heaven would take nine days and nights to reach earth, and an object would take the same amount of time to fall from earth into Tartarus. Tartarus is described as a dank, gloomy pit, surrounded by a wall of bronze, and beyond that a three-fold layer of night. Along with Chaos, Earth, and Eros, it is one of the first entities to exist in the universe."

---

[32] Retrieved online at http://www.theoi.com/Kosmos/Tartaros2.html

BRAIN DEATH

When the brain dies, your body-based-identity begins to disintegrate. As your identity is disintegrating, your senses are simultaneously expanding because the sensory limits imposed by the body are gone.

For example, human vision is frequency locked at 400-700 nanometers.

Hearing is locked at 20 Hz - 20,000 kHz.

After bodily death, sensory perception expands because the Soul is inherently sensorial, and, the senses of the body are no longer attenuating perception. This same sort of sensory expansion can happen during spiritual work, drug-induced mysticism, and Near Death Experiences.

The "invisible spiritual world" opens up to us at Death. We become telepathic and can communicate with other spiritual beings. Telepathy varies and so some Souls are more telepathic than others.

After death, colors can combine with sound, feeling, and thought in astonishing ways. Alternately, perception can become crystal clear because the "dust and noise" of the physical world is gone.

THE BARDO

When your Body-Mind dies it can no longer buffer you against spiritual realities. Food, sex, alcohol, drugs, exercise, entertainment, the internet, and all physical movement are gone. No physical stimuli exist in the Bardo.

What exists in the Bardo is the pure potency of your own Karma. There are no buffers in the Bardo; it is a pure and intense experience in Consciousness that is unmediated by any physical mechanisms.

In the Bardo people have no defenses or evasions against that which arises from their own Karma. If you live a wicked life, then you doom yourself to a Bardo that will reflect back your own wickedness to you.

This has nothing to do with any God. The Bardo is a Karmic Hall of Mirrors that reflects your true state of Consciousness back to you.

Only Truth can exist in the Bardo. The **White Light of Truth** in the Bardo pierces a Soul and reveals its interiority and secrets.

All that is hidden is made known.

The Bardo is not hallucinatory; it is revelatory and fully able to tell you the Truth about yourself.

If you cannot face the Truth about yourself in the Bardo, then the Bardo casts you out into rebirth.

In your next life you will experience the same self-deception and emotional pain that you refused to confront in the Bardo.

You are the only one who can liberate yourself.

> ➤ For evil people, the Bardo functions as Hell for it shows them how vile they really are.

> ➤ For good people, the Bardo functions as Heaven for it shows them their own Goodness.

A given transit through the Bardo is of indefinite duration because it takes as a person as long as it takes. If a person fails to confront the Truth about their true nature and repents of their sins, then Karma casts them out of the Bardo and back into rebirth.

Their rebirth will be in accord with the energy level of their Soul. This is not a caste system, for there are many very wealthy people who are very miserable. Likewise, there are people of low birth who are extraordinarily noble.

Disunified Life operates by an inflexible rule: You reap what you sow. This is the Law of Karma.

WHY CAN'T WE REMEMBER OUR PAST LIVES?

Most people cannot remember their past lives or Afterlife experiences for a very simple reason: These memories are contained in the Unconscious. Of course, these memories can be accessed using various spiritual or psychotherapeutic techniques, assuming one can move through the layers of pain, trauma, and fear that wall off the Unconscious. Not everyone can do this.

One must also accept the premise of **Surreality** to access and explore these memories. The principle is basic: Whatever arises in your exploration is whatever arises. You do not have to believe or disbelieve it. You also do not need to react to it. If some terrifying content arises, you allow it to arise and do not need to become terrified – and you will not become terrified once you realize that it is subjective content and do not identify it as belonging to you.

Follow your own curiosity and interests. Whatever content you personally find to be interesting or valuable should be looked at and considered. Whatever content holds no interest to you can be ignored.

Not everyone is interested in past lives or the Afterlife. For many people, though, it is very compelling and helps to explain and solve psycho-spiritual problems in this life. There is no rule either way about exploring past lives in Day Teaching. It is a personal decision.

I found past life exploration to be extraordinarily useful in my case. However, once I resolved past life issues, I moved on.

Past life exploration was a tactical spiritual exercise for me and not some long strategic and extended practice. I only looked at key things in my past lives that troubled me. Once those were addressed, I moved on.

THE RELIGIOUS DEAD

In the case of devoted followers of a Divinity, the angels of that Divinity conduct the Soul into a Domain of Divine Psychoactivity to meet their Divinity.

The experience of communing with one's Divinity after death is "dying and going to Heaven" in its most profound religious state. Some people receive praise while others will be judged for the life from which they just departed.

Devoutly religious people have an entirely different path following their death than do secular people. Certain religious people will get what they desired most in life. These people will fuse into their Divinity.

They will not be reborn but will instead become part of their God. This is not Eternal Life; it is Eternal Identity as part of expanding a Divinity's **God Project**. Those who have not perfected their Faith are reborn for further testing and purification. A Divinity can only fuse "Pure Souls" into their own Nature.

DIVINE JUDGMENT OF BELIEVERS

If you imperfectly served your Divinity in this life, your Divinity's essential communication to you will be that you must be reborn into the World and serve them until you attain sufficient purity to become One with them. If you agree, you are sealed to your God in the Bardo and will serve them life after life until you are pure enough to become One with them.

Many believers do this gladly.

Those who did not serve their God in life will be punished by their God per the terms of the binding spiritual contract one made while they were alive. If one agreed to be the Servant of God and did not serve but instead rebelled or blasphemed, they are held accountable.

RELIGIOUS CONVERSION AS A
BINDING CONTRACT

The words you speak in life give a Divinity a claim on you in the Afterlife. For this reason, you must formally and verbally renounce your God while you are alive if you no longer believe or desire to serve.

It is imperative to leave a religion while you are alive and in the body. Doing so frees your Bardo from the claims of a Divinity; this although your Bardo will be colored by your religious practice in life.

Communion with a Divinity during your lifetime opens a person to the influence of the Divinity and that of other believers, angels, and departed believers who died in faith. The major religions of the World are made of extraordinarily long collective chains that span both the physical and spiritual universes.

Once a person's Consciousness has been converted to the identity of a "Servant of God" it becomes very hard to unconvert.

This is why the Apostle Paul warned Christians that it is better to never be saved than to be saved and then walk away.

This type of warning is common to religious practices:

> *People can know our Lord and Savior Jesus Christ and escape the world's filth. But if they get involved in this filth again and give in to it, they are worse off than they were before. It would have been better for them never to have known the way of life that God approves of than to know it and turn their backs on the holy life God told them to live.* — II Peter 2:20-21 God's Word Translation

The Divinities play for keeps. If you freely give a Divinity power over you in this life and the next as an act of your own Will, then this forms a spiritual contract that a Divinity will assert in the Bardo.

BREAKING A RELIGIOUS CONTRACT

If you decide to break the contract – and this is your complete right to do so – then walk away completely and formally renounce your Divinity by making it known in writing and speaking.

Religions such as Christianity and Islam have long claimed a monopoly on the Afterlife and Heaven and Hell. However, as these religions are sub-Infinite, their power and control of their respective Divinities does not extend into the Afterlife except by contract.

Free Will means everything in the Spirit World. For this reason, any Divinity will always insist that you choose to be converted as an act of your own Free Will. This allows a Divinity to exert binding claims upon you and to intervene in your life by sending trials and fire.

Religious conversion is a spiritually-binding covenant. As such, it is difficult to walk away from.

I was able to walk away from Christianity because I did so early in life. I later devised and followed a very intense series of steps to formally renounce my religious conversion to Christ. Still, it took a long time to undo the code the Elohim had downloaded into me. Any form of religious conversion is Cultic. However, religions do not disclose this up front. They want people to make a decision for God in a moment of crisis when people are most vulnerable.

Persuading people to be saved when they are in crisis is Cultic on its face. Making false promises that people will be spiritually or physically healed or receive financial miracles if they will but accept God is Cultic and dishonest.

Evangelical "altar calls" are largely dishonest affairs in which intangible spiritual benefits are promised and yet frequently fail to materialize. Even worse are the televangelists who offer God's blessing to those who send money as a "seed faith" offering to God. This "seed faith scam" is such utterly ridiculous nonsense that it should be outlawed as it preys upon desperate people.

The summary of the matter is this: Unless a person explicitly agrees to cede control of their Afterlife to a Divinity, they are on their own in the Bardo. Day Teaching advocates doing your own spiritual work in this life and accumulating good Karma so that you can transit through the Bardo free from the effects of a Divinity. You can do it.

Christianity claims that people only live once and then are judged, but this is absolutely not true. It is a Christian lie told to mislead believers into thinking that Reincarnation does not exist. This in turn makes believers more amenable to giving all of their money and labor in this life to their church, as they think this life is the only life they will ever live. Christianity, however, has no power whatsoever to free a person from the Wheel of Birth and Death.

SALVATION AS FIRE INSURANCE

Some people, particularly in bygone times, embraced religious salvation as a form of "fire insurance." This meant that they accepted salvation so that they would not be sent to Hell by the "Man Upstairs" after they died. The Apostle John made it clear in Revelation 3:14-16 that Jesus detested this sort of shallow religious conversion:

> *To the angel of the church in Laodicea write: The Amen, the faithful and true Witness, the Beginning of the creation of God, says this: 'I know your deeds, that you are neither cold nor hot; I wish that you were cold or hot. So because you are lukewarm, and neither hot nor cold, I will spit you out of My mouth.*

I agree with the Holy Saint John on this one: Living a lukewarm life is a mediocre non-accomplishment. If you lead a mediocre, lukewarm existence in which you do not care about anything or bring any passion into life, then the Bardo will deem you a disappointment and send you back to yet another dreary existence until you figure out that you are responsible to make something out of your life. As the Mormons like to say, "You need to lengthen your stride!"

THRUST INTO THE WORLD

Many people are plagued by the feeling that they were thrust into this Life with no logic, reason, or necessity.

This feeling can come for many reasons, but we see it as resulting from a typical rebirth experience in which one is reborn against their will into a life that matches the energy level of their last life.

In other words, one reaps what they have sown:

❖ Live a bad life and into a bad life you will be reborn.

❖ Live a good life and you will reincarnate into a good life.

If people feel thrust into life, it is because their Karma thrust them into a concrete family setting they did not choose.

When they are young, such people often exclaim in moments of supreme frustration and anguish, "I didn't choose to be here! I didn't choose to be born!"

They are correct when they make such protests, for they did not personally choose to be here and did not consciously choose to be born.

The case is rather that their own Karma dictated their rebirth.

The opportunity in such moments of protest is to realize the Spiritual nature of Life.

The opportunity is to accept responsibility for one's rebirth and to make a vow to transcend the condition of one's rebirth.

You alone control your own Karma.

KARMA AND THE DNA FUNNEL

At the end of a Bardo transit, the Soul is pulled into the DNA Funnel and is reborn according to their Karma.

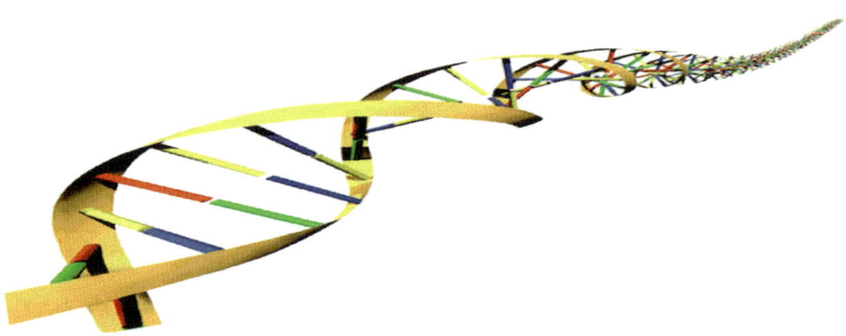

The force pulling the Soul into the DNA funnel is Disunification-Evolution. As written earlier, the Universe is a gigantic Machine of Embodiment

Thus, Karma and the DNA Funnel are interlocking and impersonal mechanisms in the Cloud of Life. These mechanisms act to ensure that Souls are appropriately reborn into embodied conditions that match their own energy level.

As part of Consciousness, Karma is a pervasive field that simply scans for conditions that match your energy level. That is how it determines where to index your Soul in the DNA Funnel. Karma uses "frequency matching" to find you a birth situation that has a comparable vibrational level to your own level.

As a general statement, Souls tend to be reborn in families, although this is not always the case. Many of us feel that we do not fit into our birth families. This may be due to the fact that we have not traveled across lifetimes with this particular bloodline.

In any case, I am one of those people who believe that your real family ultimately consists of those people whom you choose to be family.

Chapter Twenty-Eight

LIFE ON THE EDGE OF THE PSYCHO-TECTONIC PLATES

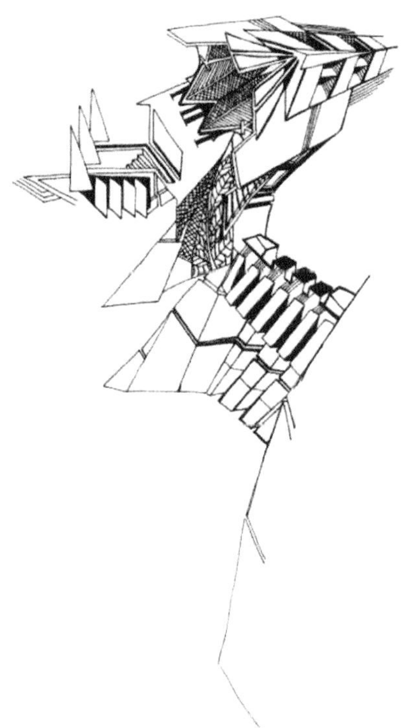

Psycho-Tectonic Plates

J. Augustine

"Cloud Mechanics" is the term for the mechanics inherent in the Disunification of Energy and Awareness.

This chapter describes striking examples of Cloud Mechanics.

The esteemed physicist John Wheeler said of the relationship of matter and space:

"Matter tells space how to curve. Space tells matter how to move."

Borrowing from Dr. Wheeler we say:

The Universe tells Consciousness where it is. Consciousness tells the Universe what it is.

Therefore –

CLOUD MECHANICS 1

EXISTENCE ITSELF

- ❖ Disunification is the possibility for Sentient Beings to exist in our Universe.

- ❖ Just as Light has a wave/particle duality, Consciousness in our Universe has a Self/Non-Self duality:

- ❖ Consciousness is to Beings what the Ocean is to drops of water. Consciousness pervades the Universe as Non-Self. Over against this are Sentient Beings.

- ❖ The descriptions of Atman, Brahma, and an Oversoul all speak to the Universal Consciousness that is not bound to any identity. This is the Transpersonal Root Consciousness of all Sentient Beings.

- ❖ Consciousness, Energy, and Matter are entangled in our Universe.

- ❖ Your Soul is an energized psychoactive space in which both the Primal Matter and Stream of Consciousness content are able to disunify and enter the World.

- ❖ Some Beings are still in the dream state, for they have not yet disunified and awakened within Disunification.

- ❖ When identity vanishes, even incrementally, relationship and spiritual enlightenment increases.

- ❖ The future of the human race is increasing relatedness and interdependence. We will emerge from past boundaries and barriers that were made out of harmful artificial identities and boundaries.

- ❖ We have entered a period wherein enormous changes in personal and collective Identity are occurring.

- ❖ The spiritual goal of Sentient Beings is to fully awaken within the physical Universe in order to realize and accomplish their full potentials.

CLOUD MECHANICS 2

RELATIVITY

Our disunified Universe is a matter of Relativity, of where you are standing as an observer.

If you are nonreligious in nature and zoom out, you may see Atheist, Zen, and Buddhist conceptions.

If you are narrowly religious and zoom in, you will see one God and embrace a Monotheistic conception.

If you are spiritually expansive and zoom out, you will see Polytheism, Pantheism, Animism, and Panentheistic points of view.

Scientifically-minded people will see natural selection and Evolution at work.

When you zoom in as close as possible, you will see Higgs bosons.

When you zoom out you will see as far as your telescopes and spectral detectors allow you to see, you will see the observable edges of the Universe.

If you go wide and see the Disunification, you will see everything.

CLOUD MECHANICS 3

SURREALITY

Day Teaching defines Surreality as follows:

Any event arising within Consciousness which has the power to challenge consensual Reality and Personal Identity

Surreality is one of the central qualities of spiritual life.

One must challenge Consensual Reality and their Personal Identity in order to do any kind of true spiritual work.

Because Day Teaching reinterprets the Unconscious as that part of the Spectrum of Consciousness that is unavailable to an individual, it logically follows that special means such as intense religious and spiritual experiences are needed to make available those portions of the Spectrum that are concerned with ultimate meanings such as life, death, and Truth.

Likewise, the same means are typically necessary to obtain entrance into those portions of the Spectrum that contain gnosis, or secret knowledge.

That Surreality attends spiritual and religious peak experiences is also to be expected inasmuch as Surreality is needed to warp and dissolve ordinary identity structures and thereby make possible the Soul's entrance into the Esoteric portions of the Spectrum.

Because souls prefer to move in groups, an esoteric entry into the Spectrum can happen on a much larger Cultural scale wherein an entire nation or people enter into a Surreal Esoteric reality that becomes expressed politically and militarily.

When this happens the World falls apart and startling new manifestations of human Consciousness and technology appear.

The Surreal Modern World in which we live is full of tremendous promise and potential even as its existing systems are being undermined and destroyed by massive fraud, corruption, and wrongdoing.

Surreality is warping and dissolving our existing models of:

- ❖ Faith and Trust
- ❖ Identity and personhood
- ❖ Money and finance
- ❖ Religion and the believer
- ❖ Sexuality and gender

And so much more.

CLOUD MECHANICS 4

PASSAGES

When you do intense spiritual work you will sometimes have – and this happens suddenly – the experience of falling apart psychologically and spiritually.

In some sense you are falling apart.

What has happened is that the psychological and spiritual "scaffolding" that holds your sense of everyday reality together is either collapsing or has collapsed entirely.

You feel lost, or even terrified, because your sense of everyday reality is gone.

You are no longer your old self. However, and this is what can be frightening, no new sense of self has arisen to replace your old sense of self.

This sort of collapse feels like a crisis but it is not actually a crisis.

It is rather a passage.

It is a passage from a lower state of Consciousness to a higher state.

You must be able understand and experience passages in order to do serious spiritual work.

During a passage, you need to focus upon the new state of freedom into which you are entering. You do not need to focus on the sense of falling apart. If you simply notice what "falling apart" feels like that is sufficient

When you know what a passage feels like you can pass more easily through them.

Passages occur throughout life and being able to recognize and handle a passage is an extremely important skill.

Newer and higher levels of Consciousness are gradually attained in spiritual work.

However, there can be incredible peak experiences and sudden jumps to higher states

 It all unfolds however it unfolds and you take it as it comes.

In enlightenment work, there are typically gradual movements punctuated by peak experiences. Some people never have peak experiences and so this is nothing to be concerned about. Such experiences happen or they don't.

Passages become bigger with each movement upward. Generally, one can only receive bigger expansions within Consciousness after first mastering smaller expansions.

CLOUD MECHANICS 5

INITIATION

That which might be considered "imaginary" by some people is quite real to others.

Moreover, any group of people can engage in a ritual that makes no sense to outsiders.

Nevertheless, ritual has great meaning internally as it corresponds to a dimension of Consciousness accessible only to initiates.

This "lock and key" system of initiation has been used for millennia as it has the effect of keeping the uninitiated away from the secrets of an inner circle.

The Primal Matter sometimes takes the form of symbols, archetypes, and dreams that are comprehensible only in terms of religious and spiritual language and experience.

Initiation is one of the ancient and proven ways in which such content can be activated.

Spiritual initiation is necessary to obtain entrance into those portions of the Spectrum that contain gnosis, or secret knowledge. Initiation is extraordinarily different from religious conversion.

That Surreality attends spiritual initiation and its attendant peak experiences is expected inasmuch as Surreality is needed to warp and dissolve ordinary identity structures and thereby make possible the Soul's entrance into the Esoteric portions of the Spectrum.

CLOUD MECHANICS 6
RECONCEPTUALIZING MENTAL CHATTER

Our natural Universe is unfiltered, noisy, and dirty. The proper response to unwanted noise and dirt is to learn how to filter it out.

Radio-astronomy is possible because so many objects in space are electrically noisy. Radio-astronomers use the term "radio-loud galaxies" to speak of galaxies powered by what are called ***retrograde black holes.***[33]

Most of us seem to have a greater or lesser degree of meaningless, chattering, intrapsychic noise that can, at times, generate anxiety and distraction inside our heads. If you have done Buddhism or Zen for some time, you have hopefully learned how to dis-identify yourself from mental chatter.

It is quite easy to recognize and filter out electrical and optical noise in electronic circuits, lasers, and other devices. It is quite another thing to learn how to recognize mental chatter for what it is, this because it is so easy to misidentify ourselves with the noise. We think the noise and chatter is some part of us we cannot get rid of.

We think we have to do something about the chatter that goes on inside of our heads. This chatter can include thoughts, images, sounds, stories, fantasies and everything else.

Day Teaching reconceptualizes mental chatter as the "unpackaging noise" of the Primal Matter unfolding itself within you. Think of it this way: Suppose you order a laptop online and have it shipped to your home. When the package arrives you want what is inside. However, you have to unpackage it first.

This means you have to carefully take apart the packaging. The packaging makes noise as you cut apart the layers of wrapping. If

---

[33] http://www.space.com/scienceastronomy/backward-black-holes-powerful-jets 100602.html

there is bubble wrap it will make popping and snapping sounds as you cut it apart. None of this unpackaging noise bothers you.

The same principle of "unpackaging noise" applies to Primal Matter as it streams into your Soul as a function of Disunification-Evolution.

All of the Primal Matter that streams into you is psychoactive. Moreover, Disunification-Evolution exerts strong unpackaging pressures in the Soul. This pressure can create intrapsychic tension.

Certain content will not be ignored. If you try to suppress such content it will simply unpackage itself in the form of physical or psychological symptoms.

The Primal Matter is a form of Spiritual Energy and something has to be done with this Energy because it cannot be destroyed.

What you do is to allow it to arise and pass through you.

Keep whatever pertains to your Soul and Destiny and release the rest.

There are endless random thoughts, images, and sensations located in the Primal Matter. This is all live streaming psychoactive phenomena. None of these phenomena belong to you but they do occur in the background of your Soul to a greater or lesser extent. Sometimes there is no unpackaging going on and it is very quiet.

Much of the Primal Matter is just random Infinite content. It is like weather passing by. The simple thing to do with this random content is to completely dis-identify with it because it is not you. It is just noise and you need to learn how to filter it out. You filter it out by not identifying with it.

All of the Primal Matter that entered our Universe had to enter in some kind of package or carrier. It was all streaming content in packages such as bosons, leptons, photons, electrons, thoughts, images, and stories. Everything in life comes in some kind of package that you have to unwrap. When you bring the groceries home from the store, there is the shuffle of bags and packages. When you open a bag of pasta or a can of soup, you mentally include the sound and do not react to it. When you peel a banana there is a slight sound and a tactile sensation that you include in the experience.

If you approach the Primal Matter in terms of Day Teaching, then you allow it all to unpackage and unfold without identifying with any of it. All you are interested in looking at is that which has meaning and purpose to you.

Once you specifically create and declare your life's central purpose, everything else becomes extraneous. You are suddenly able to filter out and ignore all of the unpackaging noise. What I am saying has to do with the Primal Matter only: I am not saying that you ignore or neglect your obligations to your body, family, creditors, or society.

A big breakthrough for me was when I reconceptualized the Eastern notion of "mental chatter" in terms of unpackaging the Primal Matter. This powerfully allowed me to restate mental chatter in terms of unpackaging pressure.

While I pay careful attention to my dream life, I also recognize that some of it is psychoactive clutter. I say this because Primal Matter uses our dreams as one of its unpackaging streams.

What you want to pay careful attention to in your dreams is content that resonates with your Soul and your purposes. There can be a great deal of tremendous information in dreams. Some dream content is based upon your daily life and some is Primal Matter. My experience is that the two can mix in dreams in such a way that allows you to gain new insights.

If you simply allow unwanted Primal Matter packaging to arise and pass, it will be liberated into the World Stream where it belongs. The key to filtering this noise is to allow it to pass through you without reacting to it. Do not falsely assign ownership of any unwanted content to yourself. Just because something pops into your head does not mean it is yours! \

CLOUD MECHANICS 7

THINGS POPPING INTO YOUR HEAD

The Spectrum of Consciousness is expanding and accelerating along with the physical Universe.

As new Primal Matter is unpackaged and unfolded, it awakens and expands into the Spectrum of Consciousness.

The Primal Matter is alive. It is psychoactive, communicative, relational, and lacks a central identity.

As it is unpackaged and released, some of the Primal Matter transits through that part of the Spectrum in which humans are frequency-locked.

The structures of the human Soul shield us from most of the Primal Matter just as the Earth's atmosphere protects it from Space.

When people take psychedelic or Consciousness-altering drugs, they bypass the protective structures and can directly experience the chaotic Primal Matter and the other parts of the Spectrum that are ordinarily unavailable to human perception.

Some small part of the psychoactive Primal Matter penetrates you and enters your own personal sense of consciousness.

It is crucial to understand that one does not need to own any strange psychoactive content that suddenly just "pops into your head" or "flashes into your imagination."

When you experience some strange transient content suddenly flashing into your head, all you need to do is to notice it, acknowledge it, and let it pass on by because it does not belong to you at all.

This psychoactive content Primal Matter craves your attention because you are the "witnessing function" for it in the same way LELA the Dreamer is the Witnessing Function for you. The

Primal Matter needs to be noticed so that it can enter the World Stream. Notice it and let it pass. Do not pay any attention to the content of its subjective chatter.

The Primal Matter is a form of energy and you can feel it.

Don't mistake its effects on your feelings as evidence of something in you.

Just notice how such content can create an effect on you.

Notice the mechanism of feeling and the tendency, or need, you feel to identify, analyze, or explain that which pops into your head.

You must learn how to decouple your tendency to identify with this transient psychoactive traffic.

This traffic is just passing through your Consciousness in the same way the weather passes over your house. Like all weather, this content may cause a temporary disturbance, or even a storm, but it will pass.

It is vital to know what belongs to you as opposed to psychoactive Primal Matter passing through.

If you have a thought or an image that is totally out of character for you then do not react to it. Do not feel guilty or somehow obligated to do anything about it. It is just a passing psychoactive fragment that grabbed your attention.

CLOUD MECHANICS 8

GENIUS & MADNESS

The midpoint between genius and madness is obsession. There is an obsessive idea or a drive to do something extraordinary.

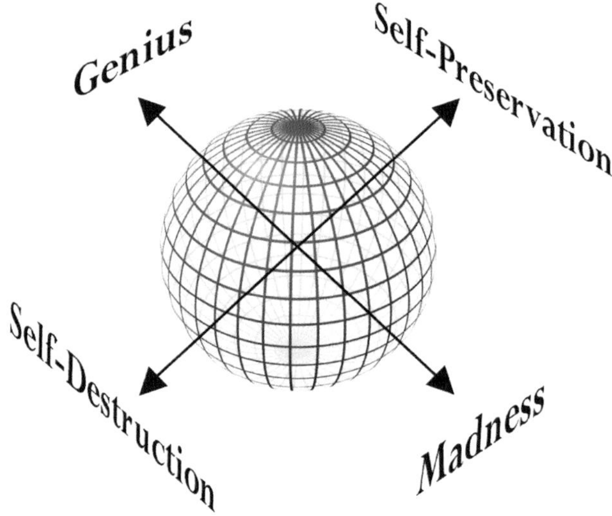

Genius implies a rare and unusual relationship to the larger Spectrum of Consciousness.

Genius, however, does not necessarily imply any other virtue.

Genius and Madness are close because the unpackaging pressures of Genius are so fast and intense that it can overwhelm a person.

Genius is like YHWH in that it is jealous and wants the Soul it inhabits to have no other Gods.

Genius and Madness are part of the range of Consciousness.

When Genius occurs in purely Personal terms it can become extremely self-destructive because the pressure of Genius is hard to bear.

Genius does not imply any other virtue. Some geniuses are terrible people. However, they are undeniably extraordinary in some particular area.

When Genius can be directed into the Transpersonal region, it can become very stable and allow for self-preservation.

We read of geniuses who have experienced singular moments of powerful world-changing insights. Some of them die early by self-destructive means whereas others die of old age.

We interpret Genius as the touch of Disunification-Evolution selectively unpackaging exceptional content within certain people who, by virtue of hard work, extraordinary talent, or highly unconventional ways of thinking are capable of understanding, developing, and particularizing rare content into forms that can be used by the World.

Nature is economical and does not waste its best stuff on people who will do nothing with it.

While Genius most definitely exists, virtually everything that is accomplished in the World occurs due to endless hours of long hard work, much of which is unseen and thankless.

CLOUD MECHANICS 9

SURREAL PHENOMENA

The Primal Matter forms the cutting edge of human Consciousness. Because the Primal Matter has no prior referents in human experience or knowledge, it's threatening, disruptive, surrealistic, and avant-garde nature typically evokes immediate resistance from the status quo.

The Primal Matter exerts incredible ***unpackaging pressures*** upon Humanity in individual and collective manifestations that include, but are not limited to surreal phenomena such as:

➤ Visions: Spiritual, technological, and futuristic

➤ New forms of Art

➤ Epiphanies

➤ Revelations

➤ Revolutionary scientific breakthroughs

➤ Disruptive new technologies

➤ The sudden and unexpected exposure of fraud and criminality

➤ Mass movements that demand Justice and the redress of grievances

➤ Bloody revolutions against fascist leaders, governments, and institutions

➤ Singular "world level" people who openly speak and teach

➤ Surrealistic experiences

➤ Apparent violations of physical or consensual realities

➤ Mystical experiences

➤ New drugs that solve old problems and create new problems

➤ Unforeseen large-scale consequences of technology

➤ UFOs and other apparently technical visitations

➤ New mass movements arising in Consciousness

An iconic 1952 grainy photograph of an alleged UFO.

One effect of these occurrences is to challenge – and ultimately abolish – existing boundaries that impede the relentless expansion of Consciousness and Technology.

Another effect of these occurrences is to expose and destroy the fraud, criminality, and injustices of the technologically enabled hyper-predators who seek to exploit and enslave the common people in order to increase their own wealth and power.

Fraud, criminality, and injustice are very often camouflaged in religious, governmental, and cultural taboos in order to better conceal themselves.

The vested interests behind fraud and criminality are the first to wave holy books, flags, and scream about their rights in fierce opposition to those who would expose them.

The status quo opposes Disunification-Evolution, particularly when it manifests as counter-culture or revolutionary defiance to the injustices of the status quo.

Artists, writers, scientists, shamans, software developers, engineers, young people and other subversives are the target audience of the Primal Matter as it seeks people who will form the cutting edge needed to dismantle taboos, constructs, boundaries, and lies that seek to impede or slow the progress of Disunification-Evolution.

The internet is now a cutting edge technological manifestation of Disunification-Evolution.

The internet is a disruptive technology capable of both unpackaging new Primal Matter content and exposing fraud and criminality.

Anonymous is a controversial manifestation of the Unconscious manifesting to fight real and perceived injustices.

For this reason, many governments, religions, and corporations want the internet gagged and muzzled when it threatens their own selfish interests.

We the People must never allow this to happen.

To paraphrase the NRA, governments and corporations can only control our internet when they pry it out of our cold dead hands.

Freedom is worth fighting for every day.

Censorship is Satanic.

Cloud Mechanics 10

The Collapse of Matrix Religious Theater

At their very top level, monotheistic religions are a form of Matrix Religious Theater; the secret of which is that God and Satan are one in the same person.

"God" is the central figure in Matrix Religious Theater.

The plotline of Matrix Religious Theater is that Good and Evil are at war. The script calls for Good to eventually win, if the faithful in the audience will persist in their belief that God is real.

God may never be suspected of having a hidden agenda. Those who come to understand God's hidden agenda are excommunicated from the Matrix Religious Theater.

Due to the power of Disunification, Matrix Religious Theater is now being systematically dismantled in its present forms. This is happening via the exposure of the hidden deviance in these theaters. It should come as no surprise to anyone, therefore, that these ancient religious theaters are collapsing.

Chapter Twenty-Nine

Earth and Moon – NASA

DAY TEACHING

The Ten Fundamental Understandings of Day Teaching are:

1. **We are Disunfied Consciousness and exist as such prior to all identities.** Whenever we get into trouble with an identity or the thoughts an identity creates, it is good to remember that all of our identities were converted from

Disunfied Consciousness. We can bypass the mechanics of identity by going directly into our pure state as Disunfied Consciousness.

2. **We can always – at any time – transcend fixed identities and self-imposed limits.** It is axiomatic in Day Teaching that a person can transcend their own self-knotted fixed identities and self-imposed limits. This can happen instantly or over time. It all depends upon how committed a person is to their fixed identities and self-imposed limits. Identities are all ultimately psycho-synthetic and can be deconstructed and transcended as you begin to dis-identify yourself with them. You are not your identity, moods, or even your beliefs. You have all of those things and none of them are ultimately you. You are ultimately disunified Awareness.

3. **We are Demiurgical.** We have the delegated power from Infinity to imagine, create, discover, invent, build, improvise, and do whatever else we need to do. We are always fundamentally creators and doers.

4. **We are Tribal.** Tribalism is inherent in human nature because we are descended from the Dream Tribes. Tribalism is powerful because Tribes have initiatory, Identity-Granting power and offer protection. In Disunity, there is no fundamental identity. Hence, the search to be initiated into an Identity-granting Tribe where one has a sense of belonging is a fundamental impulse. For many people, the highest identity is a God Tribe.

5. **We are Diverse.** Tribes naturally divide and develop distinct identities and ideologies. We are social, cultural, and organize into groups quite easily because we were once united in Infinity. Conversely, Tribes go to war with each other over many different things. War is implicit in Tribalism. Peace is a choice made between Tribes. Where Peace is not possible, there will be violence, torture, and killing. Going to war is easy. Making and keeping Peace is hard.

6. **We are Communicators, Traders, and Navigators.** The skills of communication, trading, and navigation are vital in

Disunified Life. We all need to be able to talk and listen; trade something we have to others in order for everyone to make a living; and we have to know how to navigate through whatever particular jungle we live in.

7. **We are Observers.** We have observational power to look, feel, hear, touch, taste, sense, measure, and classify. Our observations are biased. Disunification introduces countless biases into observation, demiurgical power, and Tribalism. DX Teaching ("DX" is an abbreviation for the Disunification of Energy and Awareness) works to remove as much bias as possible.

8. **We are Evolutionary**. We are forever unpackaging, expanding, and evolving. When in human form, the transpersonal forces of Physics and Consciousness unfold and expand outwards to become particularized and personalized into countless forms.

9. **We are Personal and Transpersonal**. We have the freedom to be definite, concrete personalities. We also have the freedom to be Disunified Awareness – which is the energized, psychoactive space from which all identities and persons arise.

10. **We exist both in Time and Outside of Time**. Relative to Consciousness, there is only the eternal moment of Now. Conversely, we as persons exist in time. We are completely free to shift our relationship to Time as it suits us.

Day Training is committed to helping people discover their own Primal Matter, their own True Nature, and unfold it within their lives.

In doing so, people naturally expand their Consciousness and are able to transcend fixed identities and self-imposed limits. People become much better able to realize their full talents and potentials and thus achieve their destiny.

ON THE EDGE

The World always looks likes it might spiral out of control because this could actually happen. We live on the edge of the psycho-tectonic plates where the new Primal Matter comes up from under the Unconscious.

Humanity has always lived at the raw edge of both Creation and Destruction in a highly improvisational setting.

To repeat what was written earlier:

Our situation is evident: We are limited beings arising within a situation that seldom makes sense. Why should it make sense? This is a Special Dream and these kinds of dreams seldom make sense.

You see, this place is exactly what LELA desired.

Our World is a potent, ferocious, mysterious, paradoxical, sensual realm that is completely free of the limitations of Infinity.

Look around you: there is no Unity here.

What exists is Tension, Evolution, Struggle and all of the consequences that go with the demands of survival within Disunification.

CLOUD MECHANICS 11

ENERGIZED SPACE

The Universe is a long acting time-release form of Infinity.

The purpose of the Universe is to be an energized space within which the Primal Matter can unpackage, disunify, and evolve into galaxies, stars, planets, moons, asteroids and all other physical bodies across time.

Humans are short acting time-release forms of Infinity.

The purpose of a human life is to be an energized psychoactive space within which the Primal Matter can unpackage, disunify, and evolve into all of its possibilities, this across lifetimes.

One of central purposes of human life is to create and invent in such a way that Life improves. Evolution, after all, is all about improving Life and not destroying it.

CLOUD MECHANICS 12

ENLIGHTENMENT

I created Day Teaching as way to give myself and others a way to spiritually travel higher and faster than permitted by previous spiritual vehicles weighted down by unnecessary identities, beliefs, and onerous rules of holiness and perfection that no one in this World can possibly obey.

I do not know how high or fast one can travel in terms of Enlightenment in our Universe. I have traveled very far and high and am still ascending.

Day Teaching is Infinite in nature and so bypasses all forms of conventional religion. It is necessary to do so because conventional religion has become a barrier to the Ascent and Evolution of Humanity.

A new Day is dawning in this World.

DOXOLOGY

Mother LELA says to her children:

> I birthed you in the womb
> Of the oceans of space
> My love, my Desire
>
> With wide eyes
> And open hands
> I see and feel
> For eternity's years
> I see and feel you
> You are my heart's desire.

The Children of the Day respond:

Before a step was taken in the dark, before the sky fused with the morning colors and the Day was born, before the Pharaohs sat over Egypt, there was LELA. This One moved over the face of the deep and brought forth the immensity of our Universe and everything therein.

LELA is the One who imagined the circle of the Earth in the ancient days when the glaciers carved out valleys and the oceans ran amok with fury. LELA is the One whose vision saw the beautiful range of light and the sun-kissed brown women dancing in the night. LELA is the One who evoked the Norsemen and their terrible dragon boats from the Dreaming Pool of Infinity.

LELA is the One who watches me while I sleep, who listens when I speak, and who comforts and enfolds me when I die. LELA is the breath of my soul and the sight of my eyes. This One, this One, this One is I. Feel the Mystery of LELA, the Light who existed before the Day, the very essence of dreaming and waking and this mortal play. Run out my days and nights to one hundred years and I still shall not know the Full Mystery of this One who walks the Earth in shadow and bright sunlight.

Universes without End, LELA Amen.

EPILOGUE

"Lila" is a Vedic word that refers to the Universe as the play, or the theater of God. That I call God "LELA" is my way of alluding to the Universe as a *Lila*, or as a game of God.

It is hard to be a human, but it is also a most exceptional role to assume within the Divine Theater. So be glad you were born.

Enjoy your life.

Even when it is exceptionally difficult and tragic, life is still altogether remarkable.

If you can live with purpose and courage in the face of life's adversity, then you are heroic.

LELA wants heroes. She wants people who can rise to the occasion of life and bring forth the treasures hidden within the invisible Uncreate from which we have emerged.

LELA's Lila is a Dream, a Theater, and an Astonishing Vision of Life to which you have been summoned to play a role.

APPENDIX A

LELA'S ATTRIBUTES

Day Teaching cites nine main attributes of LELA:

1. LELA exists outside of our Universe and outside of all disunified, sub-Infinite universes. LELA is Infinity.

2. Infinity is not Heaven and LELA is in no way bound to human religious descriptions or expectations. Infinity is in no way bound to the rewarding of those who held the "right" beliefs during life. Infinity is not the stronghold of firm opinion or ardent belief. Infinity will not validate any human concept of Good and Evil or any pass/fail system of morality. Infinity transcends all belief systems and so does not vindicate any belief to the exclusion of contrary beliefs. Infinity is everything and excludes nothing.

3. No sub-Infinite Religion can claim exclusive rights to Infinity based on a book, an assertion, or an enlightened person. Nor can any religious ritual or confession cause, or somehow guarantee, entrance into, or preferred status in Infinity. How could human rituals or confessions enforce a limit upon that which is limitless? Rituals and confessions represent a Limitation of Awareness rather than an understanding of Infinity. No human religion can claim Sovereignty over Infinity or claim that its sub-Infinite God brought our Universe into existence. LELA transcends the conventional God and Devil figures conceived of by the sub-infinite religions of man.

4. LELA is not the male God offered by the major monotheistic religions. LELA both encompasses and transcends human gender. God exists in a dimension in which male and female are unified within Totality. This notion is very hard for the monotheistic religions to accept inasmuch as they have been conditioned to believe that God is a male. There is no good

reason for the religious leaders of the world to maintain the fiction that God is exclusively a male and to use this fiction to continue to discriminate against women. Any thinking person will readily acknowledge that God does not have the genitals of a male human and so is therefore not a male. Being male is a biological function and not a Divine attribute. People who are unable to make this basic distinction are impoverished in many ways.

5. LELA exists outside of our Universe apart from sub-Infinite Divinities who exist in our Universe. Thus, LELA is not involved in religious and legal programs concerned with the standardization and enforcement of human morals or laws. LELA does not serve as a cosmic judge over humans. LELA does not enforce a program of omniscient, 24/7 surveillance upon the every thought, word, and deed of humans. The concept of Divine Surveillance is a creation of human Religion and not of LELA in Infinity. LELA neither endorses nor opposes human Religion.

6. LELA is not the Transpersonal-Machine of Nature. LELA transcends our physical Universe by virtue of her existence as Infinity.

7. LELA exists outside of Time, for Time is a functional attribute of sub infinite universes and not of Infinity. Time exists only when it is "Disunified from Infinity" and stably dimensionalized within the space of a bubble universe.

8. LELA caused our Universe to come into existence by a method called the Disunification of Energy and Awareness. As we mentioned, "DAY" is pronounced **Day**. It can also be pronounced **Dex** if we wish to speak of LELA shuffling the "Dex" to refer to the fact that we all have to play the hand we were dealt.

9. LELA is God only when she exists within Infinity as the absolute Unity of Energy and Awareness. When some quanta of this Unity are disunified into a bubble universe, God ceases to exist therein and atomic, subatomic and spiritual fragments of God appear instead.

APPENDIX B

THE POWERS OF INFINITY

Infinity is the ***Divine Discontentment*** that makes human art, language, religion, and mysticism possible; and yet Infinity cannot be wholly expressed by art, language, religion, and mysticism.

Infinity is the intelligence that makes human reason, logic, science, and knowledge possible, yet Infinity cannot be wholly comprehended by reason, logic, science, and knowledge.

Infinity is the Awareness that makes sub-infinite beings, dreams, and perceptions possible, yet Infinity cannot be fully incarnated, dreamed, or perceived by sub-infinite beings.

Infinity is the Energy that powers the immense galaxies of blazing stars, yet the vast galaxies themselves are but a sub-infinite fraction of the Infinite.

Infinity can be spoken of as the abode of God. However, the God who inhabits Infinity is not the God who cannot tolerate the worship of golden calves or sexual excess. The Law and the Prophets do not define the One in Infinity. That One is neither bound by the teachings of the prophets and priests nor to the neurotic demands of their followers. This One cannot be codified or reduced to doctrinal statements. LELA does not need human praise or worship – as if human acknowledgement could somehow affirm, validate, or improve upon the condition of Infinity.

Infinity is the Fiery Domain of God and not the luxuriant eternal-retirement community depicted in the New Testament. The One who inhabits Infinity is idolatry and sexual excess; this One is the Law and the Prophets; this One is the souls of the dead, the crying infants, and the sacred books. All contradictions are unified in Infinity and expressed in Disunity.

Infinity is the flux an inexhaustible imagination from which all sub-infinite forms, processes, and beings arise. Infinity is afire with LELA's inexhaustible imagination and from her imagination radiate endless possibilities, beings, worlds, and universes.

You and I are among the countless forms, processes, and beings that have been imagined by Infinity. You existed in the Dreams of God before you were formed and even before our Universe was formed. In Day Teaching, LELA and Infinity are synonymous.

Infinity is clearly not about the idiotic delusions of the pompadoured men and the weepy, big-haired women who inhabit the baroque slums of religious television. Rather, Infinity is about the tension and creative agony of an inexhaustible imagination.

Once one understands God as Infinity, one must surrender both the happy fictions and nightmarish judgments of human Religion.

Infinity does not care about your bank account, personal safety, or death. This is a hard truth for believers to accept, particularly when they have been brainwashed by the Prosperity Gospel and other religious lies.

GLOSSARY

Abrahamic Monotheism: The main monotheistic religions of the world are Judaism, Christianity, and Islam. Because these three religions all began with the biblical patriarch Abraham, they are thus said to be branches of ***Abrahamic Monotheism***. Monotheism maintains that only one Supreme Creator-God exists and that all lesser gods and goddesses are false and Satanic in nature. See *Monotheism*.

Afterlife and Accountability: The spiritual belief that an Afterlife exists in which the newly dead are held accountable for the lives by God, Karma, or agents of God such as Archangels.

Akashic Records: From Wikipedia: "The (Akasha is a Sanskrit word meaning "sky," "space" or "aether") are said to be a collection of mystical knowledge that is stored in the aether; i.e. on a non-physical plane of existence. The concept is common in some New Age religious groups. The Akashic Records are said to have existed since the beginning of Creation. Just as we have various specialty libraries (e.g., medical, law), there are said to exist various Akashic Records (e.g., human, animal, plant, mineral, etc). Most writings refer to the Akashic Records in the area of human experience." In Day Teaching, the Cosmic Mandala is understood to instantly record everything in the Universe as it happens. This recorded data can be called the Akashic Records.

Annihilation Horizon: In Day Teaching, the Annihilation Horizon is the boundary region between Infinity and a virtual *new Universe* (nU). At the Annihilation Horizon, a virtual new Universe must either disunify into an actual sub-Infinite Universe or collapse back down into Infinity. See *Black Pearl* and *nU*.

Archetypes: As used in this book, *archetypes* refer to those primal energies of Consciousness that were disunified from Infinity during the Disunification of Energy and Awareness. For a description of archetypal energies, see definitions of *Divinities, Many Energies, dATable,* and *Sha* in this glossary.

Arising: This word refers the totality of that which is manifest and appears in our Universe and within you. You can generally see, feel, measure, know, and experience most of that which is arising within yourself and the world around you. To the extent that you cannot see or know that which is arising, you are unaware.

Black Pearl: A virtual *new Universe* (nU) consisting of super-condensed *Primal Matter.* A Black Pearl is a new Universe positioned at the *Annihilation Horizon.* As such, a Black Pearl must either disunify into an actual sub-Infinite Universe or collapse back down into Infinity. See also *Annihilation Horizon, Chromacolor Condensate, Disunification of Energy and Awareness,* and *nU.* In human life, any person is said to be in a condensed "Black Pearl state" when they are on the "tense edge" of a great life event that will either become a breakthrough into a new state of life or a collapse back into their existing life. A Black Pearl state demands a monumental, life-changing decision. There is no escaping from the decision or its consequences.

Celestial Hierarchy: The belief that God presides over a Celestial Hierarchy that includes Angels, Demons, Humans, and other Entities.

Chromacolor Condensate: A Black Pearl that has crossed over the **Annihilation Horizon** and is actively disunifying into a new Universe. The term **Chromacolor Condensate** refers to the first primal physical structures, or Primal Matter, that "condense" or "disunify" out of Infinity during the first billionths of seconds of the Disunification of Energy and Awareness:

- ❖ Disunified Consciousness
- ❖ Source codes
- ❖ Fundamental Forces
- ❖ Force Carriers
- ❖ Higgs Bosons

This notion of a ***primordial structural condensate*** evokes the Sanskrit notion of "Maya" or the invisible, psycho-synthetic structure within which visible, disunified universes manifest.

Consciousness: The fundamental human experience of being alive, sentient, and intelligent. See also *disunified Awareness* and *dATable*.

Cosmic Mandala: The Cosmic Mandala is the Cosmic Matrix of Supercomputers, the operating system of which is the Source Codes of Disunification. The data the Cosmic Mandala will record has been called the ***Akashic Records.*** When our Universe begins, the Cosmic Mandala pervades the Cosmos via universal forces and fields. The Mandala instantly records everything in the Universe as it happens.

Creation Ex Nihilo: The Catholic doctrine that the God of the Bible created the material Universe from nothing by speaking matter into existence. The doctrine of *Creation Ex Nihilo* further argues that absolutely nothing existed before God created our Universe. Therefore, there was no pre-existent matter, spirits, angels, universes before ours. This is because Genesis 1:1 says, "In the beginning God created the Heavens and the Earth." St. Augustine strictly held that Genesis 1:1 recorded the "first beginning" of everything.

dATable: When Disunification occurs, disunified Awareness is converted into many different expressions of Consciousness. These forms are listed in the "dATable" discussed and shown on pages 109-110**. The dATable is a chart showing examples of the "discrete forms of Consciousness" into which Disunified Energy was converted during the Disunification of Energy and Awareness.

Day Rise Trinity Explosion: The explosion in the Black Pearl that triggered the Disunification of Energy and Awareness. The Black Pearl was annihilated and released its condensed Primal Matter was initially released as the ***Chromacolor Condensate.***

<u>Day Teaching</u>: The alternative to Divine Creation and the Big Bang is the Disunification of Energy and Awareness. *Day Teaching* and *Day Teaching* are synonymous with *Day Teaching.*

<u>Day Teaching</u>: This term refers to Day Teaching as a fusion of Technology and Mysticism.

<u>Disunification of Energy and Awareness</u>: 1. Infinity is the Life Energy/Life Awareness existing in Unity. The Disunification of Energy and Awareness is a high-energy, faster-than-light event in which some small fraction of Infinity is disunified into a sub-Infinite universe and all of the forms, processes, and beings in it. The DAY event that initiated our Universe would look like a "Big Bang" on this side of the Universe, for we cannot observe the pre-universe DAY states of the *Chromacolor Condensate* or the *Black Pearl.* The Disunification of Energy and Awareness is a process that happens endlessly in Infinity as new universes are constantly spawned. The "Disunification of Energy and Awareness" is variously referred to as "The DAY" or "The Disunification" within this book.

Below are the key definitions related to the *Disunification of Energy and Awareness*, or *DAY*:

- **<u>Disunfied Awareness</u>**: Infinity is the Life Energy/Life Awareness existing in Unity. When Disunification occurs, the "Life Awareness" aspect of Infinity is disunified into a Disunified Awareness. "dA" is the abbreviation for Disunified Awareness. When Disunification occurs, disunified Awareness is converted into the many different expressions of Consciousness. These forms are listed in the "dATable" discussed and shown on pages 147-148**. The dATable is a chart showing examples of the "discrete forms of Consciousness" into which Disunified Energy was converted during the Disunification of Energy and Awareness.

- **<u>Disunified Energy</u>**: Infinity is the Life Energy/Life Awareness existing in Unity. When Disunification occurs, the "Life Energy" aspect of Infinity is disunified into a

Disunified Energy. **dE**: The abbreviation for Disunified Energy. When Disunification occurs, disunified Energy is converted into the physical elements.

Day: The term "Day" is an abbreviation for the Disunification of Energy and Awareness. Instead of writing "the Disunification of Energy and Awareness" each and every time, we use an abbreviated term: "Day."

Day Dream: A special "Dream of God" in which LELA dreams of new and unique universes.

DaySphere: An empty space, or void, inside of which sub-Infinite universe is located.

DayVerse: A sub-Infinite universe.

Disunification: The process whereby Infinity spawns sub-infinite universes in the Multiverse.

Disunification-Evolution: ("Day-Ev") Disunification-Evolution is the relentless force of Evolution that continually unpackages, self-assembles, and evolves the Primal Matter of our Universe. Disunification-Evolution evolves simplicity into complexity.

Day-Ev: The short form of ***Disunification-Evolution***.

Divinities: A term referring to all of the sub-Infinite Gods and Goddesses in our Universe. Day Teaching prefers and uses the gender-neutral term "Divinities" as opposed to the older terms of "Gods and Goddesses."

Domains of Divine Psychoactivity: The Divinities have historically told humans that they, the Divinities, live in Heaven. The location of Heaven has always been abstract and is usually referred to being located somewhere up in the Sky. Being non-physical, the Divinities exist in another dimension that is somehow entangled in our dimension. I experience the Divinities as Energies that I feel in my body. I call the dimension in which the Divinities live the *Realm of Divine Psychoactivity*. I conceive of this Realm as being a vast dimension of Disunified Consciousness that is full of numberless states of Consciousness. Divine energies, Sha energies, and the energies of deceased humans and animals populate this Realm. The Realm of Divine Psychoactivity is a reflection of the entire Energies resident within. This Realm is a Constant Flux of Consciousness pervaded by Egos, Chaos, and Endless Images.

Dream Tribes: LELA's Demiurgi. Their job is to harvest the Primal Matter, or raw materials, from Infinity that are needed to turn LELA's DAY Dream into an actual universe. There were nine Dream Tribes that worked on our Universe. Below are shown the functions of LELA's Dream Tribe when they worked in the Mystery-Land of the pre-Universe:

- Dream Tribe I: The Dream Tribe Masons (DTM) quarried the Quarkatype.

- Dream Tribe II: The Fundamental Interactions

- Dream Tribe III: Pre-Scribing Infinity into Particles and Wavelengths

- Dream Tribes IV & V: The Programmers of the Source Codes of Disunification

- Dream Tribe VI: Communications and Interfaces

- Dream Tribe VI: The Hall of Records

- Dream Tribe VIII: Embodying the Dreamer

- Dream Tribe IX: Initiated the process of the Disunification

During the DAY, the Dream Tribes were disunified into the sub-Infinite *Divinities*.

DX: The term "DX" is an abbreviation for the Disunification of Energy and Awareness.

Elohim: A plural word in Hebrew. In Day Teaching "The Elohim" are considered to be a discarnate, non-human group of Divinities, or Higher Intelligences, that are committed to enforcing their Judeo-Christian morality upon Humanity. YHWH, or Yahweh, is the leader of The Elohim.

Embodiment: Day Teaching understands the Machine of Nature is a gigantic packaging machine that endlessly packages quanta in all manner of neatly packaged forms, processes, and beings as dictated according to the *Source Codes of Disunification*. See also *Synthetic Unities*.

Final Inrush: The *Day Rise Trinity Explosion* was triggered by the *Final Inrush* of Power from Infinity. This Final Inrush was the last, and largest, single contribution of Energy from *Infinity* into our Universe. For narrative purposes, we conceive of the Final Inrush happening one attosecond before the Day Rise Trinity Explosion. The inrush thus caused the *Day Rise Trinity Explosion* detonation.

Gate: The Gate between Infinity and our bubble Universe was open for 10^{-18} of a second, or one attosecond. During this time, the sum total of the *Primal Matter* needed to provision our Universe was transferred from Infinity. This high capacity, high-energy, highly stable transfer resulted in the massive *Day Rise Trinity Explosion* detonation. This is the process of how Disunification converts some part of Infinity into universes.

God: In DAY[34] Teaching, "God" is understood to exist as Infinity rather than existing within the confines of any SpiritMatter religion. The Infinite God is understood to exist outside of our sub-Infinite Universe. God is Infinity and not a glorified human person, an eternal person, or a SpiritMatter God. "God" is a placeholder name for now. Day Teaching asserts that Infinity has two components: **Life Energy** and **Life Awareness**. These two components are bound into a State of Unity. This Unity is Infinity – or God, if you prefer. The acronym for the ***Life Energy/Life Awareness*** is ***LELA***. This feminine personification of God is intended to counter the masculine, brutal magnificoes that populate monotheism. Infinity is not our Universe, but rather surrounds and contains our Universe and countless other universes. Day Teaching therefore describes multiple universes, or what is also called a Multiverse.

---

[34] "DAY" is the abbreviated form of the "Disunification of Energy and Awareness." This is the technical-mystical event that caused the Big Bang. The term "Day Teaching" simply refers to my body of teaching about the Disunification of Energy and Awareness.

Infinity: The sum total of all *Life Energy/Life Awareness* unified into One. Infinity is the flux an inexhaustible imagination from which all sub-infinite forms, processes, and beings arise. Infinity is afire with LELA's inexhaustible imagination and from her imagination radiate endless possibilities, beings, worlds, and universes. You and I are among the countless forms, processes, and beings that have been imagined by Infinity. In Day Teaching, LELA and Infinity are synonymous. Pages 53-55** offer the key definitions of Infinity used in this book.

Infinity-Divinity: A term for LELA TAO as the One in Infinity. In Day Teaching, LELA TAO is God; she is the One *Infinity-Divinity*. All of the Divinities in our Universe are sub-Infinite and form part of a Pantheon.

Infinity Surround: The space immediately on the outside of a sub-Infinite universe. The Infinity-Surround physically contacts Infinity in the same way that the upper boundary of Earth's atmosphere physically contacts outer space.

LELA: An acronym for Life Energy/Life Awareness. In Day Teaching, LELA is Infinity; she is the sum total of all Life Energy and Life Awareness unified into One.

During the Disunification of Energy and Awareness, LELA was disunified into our Universe and everything in it. See *God*.

LELA LTD: LELA LTD is the name of LELA when she is sleeping and dreaming of new universes. LTD is an acronym for *"LELA the Dreamer."* When LELA dreams, she loses her knowledge of Infinity and surrenders herself into the Dream. When this happens, her Dream Tribe appears.

LELA TAO: LELA TAO is the name of LELA when she exists as the One in Infinity. TAO is an acronym for *"The Awakened One."* Hence, LELA TAO is the Awakened Divine One in Infinity.

Maya: A Sanskrit word meaning veil or illusion. The Sanskrit notion is reconceptualized in Day Teaching: See *Psycho-Synthetic* and *Psycho-Synthetic Reality Process*.

Monotheism: Monotheism is the belief that there is only one true God who created the Universe and Humanity. Monotheism comes from ***mono***, which means one, and theism, which means God. Hence, Monotheism is the belief that there is only one God. The main monotheistic religions of the world are Judaism, Christianity, and Islam. Because these three religions all began with the biblical patriarch Abraham, they are thus said to be branches of ***Abrahamic Monotheism***. Monotheism maintains that only one Supreme Creator-God exists and that all lesser gods and goddesses are false and Satanic in nature.

Multiverse: In Day Teaching, a Multiverse is defined as the idea that Infinity spawns innumerable universes into a collective that can be called the Multiverse. Each universe can have different physics and sets of rules.

Mystery-Land: The place in which LELA's DAY Dreams take place. Human dreams also take place in a Mystery-Land. Mystery Land is therefore a transitional boundary region that allows great changes to occur in its protective shadow. Mystery Land is both the place and the condition in which Pandora can disunify Infinity in order to explore the Extreme Mysteries of Non-Infinities while LELA TAO pervades and maintains the Unity of Infinity. The Full Moon is the Symbol of Mystery Land.

nU: An abbreviation meaning "new Universe." In Day Teaching, a nU is a virtual object; it is a new Universe on the edge of disunifying into an actual, sub-Infinite universe or collapsing back into Infinity. See also *Annihilation Horizon* and *Black Pearl*.

Pandora: Another name for LELA TAO.

Pantheism: The belief that God pervades and suffuses all forms, processes, and beings. God is in all and through all.

Paradox of Infinity: Because Infinity is the totality of everything, no separate thing can exist therein. In Infinity, everything exists simultaneously in Unity. There is no distinction between the personal and the transpersonal, light and darkness, or an idea and its expression. There is only the Unity of God, and no separate thing can stand out over against that Unity. LELA thus suffers the stunning, paradoxical limitation of Infinity: There can be no Creation within Infinity since it must remain an undifferentiated Unity.

<u>Polytheism</u>: The belief that many Gods and Goddesses exist in a Celestial Hierarchy.

<u>Psycho-Synthetic</u>: In Day Teaching, Infinity is understood to be an Absolute Unity, or One. Because Disunification happens outside of Infinity, it is therefore synthetic; it being axiomatic in Day Teaching that, "Absent Unity, there can only be Synthesis."

<u>Psycho-Synthetic Reality Process</u>: The collective sub-Infinite processes that generate all synthetic, sub-Infinite Realities outside of Infinity. *PSRP* is the acronym for the *Psycho-Synthetic Reality Process*. It is axiomatic in Day Teaching that, "Absent Unity, there can only be Synthesis." All forms, processes, and beings in our universe arise as the sum of numberless syntheses and interactions occurring in, and across, Time. See also *Cosmic Mandala*, *Source Codes of Disunification*, and *Maya*.

<u>Primal Matter</u>: The raw materials that the Dream Tribe Demiurgi harvests from Infinity in order to turn a Day Dream into a universe.

<u>Quarkatype</u>: A word formed by compounding the words *Quark* and *Archetype*. This coined word is used to indicate that the stones the Dream Tribe hews from Infinity are composed of the very Life Energy and Life Awareness of Infinity itself. During the Disunification, these stones became the *Primal Matter*, or *primal matter*, that formed our Universe.

<u>Reincarnation</u>: Some, but certainly not all, religions believe that the soul reincarnates in order to achieve a spiritual education. When Perfection is attained, the soul is freed from the Wheel of Birth and Death.

<u>Soul</u>: Day Teaching defines a Soul as Consciousness converted into an Identity. An Identity is defined as an "I" that experiences its own self-existence. Conversely, Consciousness does not experience itself as an "I" but rather simply observes all things in the arising phenomenal Universe. While Consciousness pervades the Universe, Souls do not.

Source Codes of Disunification: The operating system for our Universe that was uploaded into the Cosmic Mandala. The Primal Matter harvested from Infinity by LELA's Dream Tribe was formed into the Source Codes of Disunification.

SpiritMatter: The conceptual medium used to construct certain religions.

Synthetic Unities: Day Teaching maintains that, absent the Unity of Infinity, there can only be *Synthetic Unities*. The corollary to this is that Absent Unity, there can only be Entropy. Our Universe is a large-scale synthetic unity. All of the forms, processes, and beings in our Universe are embodied as smaller synthetic unities, temporal bodies that energetically emerge and appear in spacetime. All synthetic unities and temporal bodies eventually collapse down due to Entropy.

Uncreate: The Uncreate is Infinity that has not yet been disunified into Primal Matter in order to source a universe.

Unconscious: Two things occur by default when the Soul knots itself into existence. The first thing that occurs is that the Soul becomes blind to the ***larger Spectrum of Consciousness*** out of which it has knotted itself. Day Teaching recasts the ***Unconscious*** as those parts of the Spectrum of Conscience that are normally inaccessible to a Soul.

§

Made in the USA
Charleston, SC
15 October 2013